KIND REGARDS

(LIFE OF THE EXTRAORDINARY ORDINARY)

A.N.M. SWEENEY

Copyright © A.N.M. Sweeney in 2021

Published by DrewCat Publishing

Paperback ISBN-13: 978-1-7398790-0-6
eBook ISBN-13: 978-1-7398790-1-3

Printed in the United Kingdom

Cover design and layout by www.spiffingcovers.com

To those who love me, please don't read this.

Seriously, Mum, Dad, don't read it.

Before we begin

"You're really nothing special."

This sentence haunts me. Why would she say it? Did she mean I'm not as great as I think I am, or that I'm nothing? These four words are ingrained into my mind. They can pop up at any moment, such as the moment that led to the idea of this book. There I was, standing alone at a rave, in an abandoned warehouse, on a cold Easter Sunday. I stood next to two perfectly sculpted ravers with nothing but chains and leather covering their glistening flesh. Both in a delirious state, they throttled each other's shaved heads as they attempted to eat each other's faces, like two hippos fighting over a watermelon. I remained still, glancing every so often to make sure they wouldn't knock me off my feet. I'd peek out the corner of my eye and be drawn to the redness of theirs, bloodshot from the amphetamines they'd bombed, snorted, or injected. I don't know what they were on or why I was there, but there I stood thinking this couldn't be it. This isn't what life is. This really isn't special.

I've written this to show life from my perspective as the extraordinarily ordinary, existing in London, where else? I see life as a stage full of performers, people in costumes playing their part. We're trapped in a web of overlapping stories each trying to write our own fairy tale. I feel like I couldn't be further from my comfortable childhood in pretty Liverpool, where any issue I faced could be sorted by asking my parents, or people around me; all problems would disappear.

One of my first school memories is a perfect example – my first school sports day, aged four (they started us pretty young). We were sat pitchside, being told the proceedings of the sports day, probably something as simple as when we'd be getting up for the sack race. All we had to do was sit down and listen to our teacher, Mr Buckley. I sat down and shrieked. I had gone to rest my weight on my arms but got such a shock when I didn't feel the dry grass as expected. I somehow managed to put my hand into a dog turd that could have filled a shoebox. I've no idea how everybody missed it, well, almost everybody. Being four years old, I yelped and burst into tears (I was such a crier, still am). The teachers heard my cry and I was immediately tended to. Another teacher rushed to me, took me by my clean hand, and walked me to a toilet to help wash away the excrement. Within two minutes the crisis had been resolved; all I had to do was whinge. I didn't think this life would end. I'd never envisaged my screams not being tended to, nor having to wash dirt off myself. Nor did anybody tell me just how much dog shit there is in the real world. Welcome to my attempt at coming to grips with the harsh lessons of life.

If you're looking for inspiration, try reading Harry Potter instead.

Life is like needing a piss in the middle of the night. Even though you'd rather stay in your comfort zone, it's necessary to do something. If you stay in bed, things won't get better; it could get smelly and the stains of the mattress won't wash away (and the landlord will make sure you don't get your deposit back). So you stumble to the toilet, blindly feeling your way round in the hope you don't stub your toe or smack your shins. Once you get there it's anyone's game. Fire away and hope for the best; use your eyes and ears to the best of your ability. It'll work out in the end. Good luck.

I only have a sit-down wee on a hangover.

Through the teachings of life so far, I've learned to deal with my own emotions, which has caused me to develop an overpowering sense of self-awareness. I wish I didn't possess it. I have thus chosen to channel my emotions from my observations and experiences into here. I bury my feelings into this book, to enable me to play the carefree fool and carry on without my brain imploding. I cannot express my emotions to the world around me; I must allow people to continue to be ignorant. I wouldn't want to bother them; they've got their own problems to deal with. We all do. Nevertheless, I try to see the funny side of it all, because I have to laugh or I'll die and I don't think I want to die.

London Town

The Big Smoke, where the money is. I've always wanted to make something of myself, to be recognised in some way (once I accepted being a footballer wouldn't happen, not that I'm bitter). I spent much of my late-teens stressing every night as I planned my route to get to this hub of opportunity. After all, it is home to the big banks, tech titans, huge hedge funds and marketing mammoths – if you can name them (give or take a few based over in Ireland for one reason or another, wink-wink), they're in London; I knew I had to be too. Having been here for four years, I have seen how great this city is. Such a diverse population who are among the brightest and most innovative in the entire world, and who are not only allowed but encouraged to create and test their abilities to their maximum. Yet, everybody seems so miserable here. Living in this city is such a unique experience because of the overpopulation, the nature of the work and, above all, the glamour. The city promises so much and, as a result, traps many.

I'm still here.

It didn't take long for me to convince myself the so-called better work was in London (thanks to my Dad constantly telling me this in my teenage years). I thought I'd have the potential to earn more and somehow presumed I'd thrive in a higher pressured environment, despite never really experiencing one. London would enable me to force myself to where I've always wanted to be, though I have no idea where that is.

Nobody told me that I'd be as insignificant as I am in the real world; a lesson I have struggled to learn, being such an attention seeker. Nobody told me it would take me two years to be invited to a business meeting. Nobody said my existence would be to appease the lives of those in higher positions than my own. I thought this was the city of expression and opportunity, not spending each day anxious to know whether I'm acknowledged or not. Alas, here I am. I go to bed each night dreading the coming morning. I lie in bed struggling to sleep because of my hideous mood. I can do nothing but stare at a slim rectangular window, which is not square to the wall (maniac architect ruining my life), listening to people threatening to take each other to court over weed money.

What is this life?

Chapter I – Where am I?

Good morning, to me

Yes, that's right, beginning with the ultimate cliché, but where better to start? Like so many, I am not a morning person. What's not to hate about mornings? Particularly when waking up for a job you don't want to get out of bed for (it's worth me noting that I can't quit my job, I have to obtain my qualification and complete a year of post-qualification before another employer will look at my CV; we'll get to that).

Mornings begin with an alarm piercing my brain and dragging it from its slumber. Every morning I'm yanked away from dreaming of another life, a different purpose, possibly a different lover – oops. I know, I cannot control them. If I could, I wouldn't give myself the headache of trying not to act weird the morning after the night before. I'm referring to the experience of waking to the horrific feeling of guilt after dream cheating. We've all felt it. When you're single and have these dreams, it feels only slightly strange and soul-crushing. These feelings subside after a five-minute stalking of your one-night stand's Instagram page while your body wakes up. You can do what you want with that. But when un-single, dream cheating is a different ball game.

It felt so much worse the first time round. When I woke from my dream, it took me about 30 seconds to register where I was because the dream had been so vivid. Then it hit me; I was a dirty no-good trollop. My mind instantly craved some reassurance, *No one would even know*, I told myself, *It's not as if you've actually done anything bad.* I'd just been in a supermarket on a date with Emilia Clarke, it was terrible. If any person or search engine could reliably explain the above, please do as it would soothe my conscience. I was helpless. It became a mental battle of will to convince myself that I am in fact a decent human being, despite experiencing dreams about going out with people I don't even know, while my girlfriend lay next to me dreaming of daffodils, fairies, and absolutely not penis.

I continued to reassure myself. It's fascinating how we can perform this trick on our own minds. When faced with self-doubt we have the ability to praise ourselves, for we are exemplary in our behaviour. We are. If something we've done makes us feel anxious (wait until we actually get to the warehouse rave), or if we've acted irrationally, surprising ourselves; we forgive ourselves over time, eventually forgetting all. Magic is real. We don't even notice the feeling of guilt pass. We wake up one morning and the monkey once clinging to our backs has left without saying goodbye; how wonderful.

As I came to grips with the morning guilt from my first time, the alarm began to shriek again. Now having fully woken up from the dream of infidelity, I peered across to my lady companion lying next to me. She looked back through one half-opened eye, no doubt confused herself having been awoken probably from a dream involving a real man, not daffodils. She gave me a look to show something was making her uneasy, which made me realise the alarm had been blaring out for almost half a minute. She mustered her strongest attempt at a smile (I'd pretend to make a joke about it showing how long ago this was and that I don't see her smile every morning, but she still smiles at me every morning, which makes this all the worse).

I returned as insincere a smile as I've ever given. Behind

the smile was guilt mixed with fear. I was looking at her in her half-opened eye having spent the night out with another. What if she'd have found out, or the dream world version of Emilia Clarke found out I had a girlfriend? What an impossible situation to deal with. I'm now an expert in handling this emotion, not that it happens particularly often (only three times a week). I've discovered performing complex maths multiplications in my head works (the ability to do so comes in handy in all kinds of situations). If only we could somehow control our dreams, rather than wake up in cold sweats because we have spent a night dreaming about someone or something we shouldn't. Waking up to think, is it love? Lust? Is it an obsession? One thing I will say about these voodoo mind tricks, for all the guilt and negativity, at least they take my mind off reality.

Without these dreams my life is mundane. Every morning, I'm battling to sleep against this deafening siren coming from my phone. Blinding all of my senses with one massive foghorn. I can't think straight; my head throbs and the contents of my skull feel like a bottle of Diet Coke having been mixed with mentos (if you don't know what that looks like, you can have some fun on YouTube later). I turn back to hit the snooze button to put my mind at rest, but I've convinced myself I won't get brain cancer if I sleep with the phone an extra two feet away from me on the floor around the far side of the bedside table, as opposed to on it. I'm aware this is moronic beyond belief, but I am unable to sleep without the radiation shield I've imagined my bedframe gives me. I therefore have to shuffle my entire body to the edge of the bed and throw my hand towards the phone to flick snooze. My first exhausting task of any day, can it get any worse? Flinging myself towards the phone proves to be a grave error as it exposes my body to the freezing cold air still lingering from the night. It floods under the duvet and clings to my body, making everything worse.

I'm faced with two options:

Option one: admit defeat. I'm going to get up anyway. I am now awake. I can hurl my legs towards the wall hoping my body follows, after all, the shower is waiting to warm me up (personally, I think this depends on the quality of the shower, which we will get to).

Option two: I can wrap myself into the duvet, which involves driving my shoulder down into the pillow to propel myself like an alligator (or is it a crocodile?) attacking its prey, thus allowing the duvet to cloak me and begin the toasting process. The fundamental issue with this is that the warmer I become, the drowsier I get and I begin to drift away again. My head is flooded with a numbing sensation as I lie on the edge of a deep sleep, atop the pinnacle of relaxation. I quickly return to limbo. I am weightless and feel nothing; it is truly wonderful. For a short moment, I feel complete euphoria. A short moment, which is quickly destroyed by the second wave of attack from the alarm, and here I am facing a near carbon copy situation that I faced, in my case, nine minutes ago.

I hate mornings.

Despite the hatred, I tend to persevere with option one. I'll sling myself out of bed, but before I head for the shower, I must seek out water. My mouth dries out every night to the point where I'm left with an unbearable thirst. It's as if I've consumed a bag of salt in my sleep; it is vile. The worst part is that I can taste how pungent the dryness causes my breath to smell. I clutch at my frosted pint glass of room temperature water (yes, I leave myself one every night. Stay hydrated) from the bedside table and press it to my mouth, drinking like a dog on a hot day. I slurp it so quickly that the water flows outside the rim of the glass where it meets the corners of my mouth, causing the water to flow down my chin, before dripping down to my abdomen. It still shocks me a little as it makes contact, even though I know it's coming. Determined, I tilt my head backward to empty the remainder of the glass, exhaling heavily immediately after I swallow, allowing my body the chance to gasp for oxygen and enable me to pucker my lips and mutter the first words of any given day, "Ah, fuck sake."

A long shower in the morning is what kick-starts my day, unless, of course, it's a tin-pot shower. If you're unfortunate enough to have a bathroom ruined by a bath with a stand-in shower as your option, search elsewhere immediately. You need an attractive standalone with space to lunge for those morning groin stretches. In central London, just shy of £3,000 per month pays enough for a one bathroom stand-in shower that will make you reassess if the life you're leading is worth such suffering. A shower has to be a sanctuary, where life-changing decisions are made. It's the theatre where we rehearse the most meaningful conversations we have, where people decide if they'll give their relationship another chance or make the new job application they've been thinking about. The shower must be a place that inspires; a haven for us to seek asylum when overwhelmed with many of life's problems from which we emerge the most fresh-faced and motivated version of ourselves. We owe it to ourselves to have a great shower in the morning. What have I got? A bathroom no bigger than a broom cupboard that comprises of a bath built for a guinea pig with a stand-in shower.

Cheers.

Not exactly inspiring, but it does the job – for now. I can clear my head and get ready for the full morning ritual. We each have our own; routines that we've crafted and perfected with each passing morning, which we subconsciously train ourselves to carry out, as we prepare for, no doubt, a strenuous day ahead. Mine doesn't involve anything too out of the box, merely a full stretch, followed by a full-body moisturising after my shower, some facial moisturiser to rehydrate, followed by factor 50 on my face to give me a glow and protect me from the sun on my pale face. Admittedly I read it prevents wrinkles too, though my forehead could do with a few drops of Botox.

After dressing myself (thankfully I only have to wear suits for days I have meetings, which isn't too often), I'll brush my teeth twice; once for the entire mouth then an extra 30 seconds dedicated to my front six pearls. They need to be ultra-white for when I leave. Thankfully my hair seems to fall into place after a ten-second blast with a hair dryer. It only takes me an hour from getting up to leaving the flat. Somehow I have friends who can do it in 15 minutes, but I have no idea where I can make up the time; my ritual is sacred. I'll head for the door with zero optimism for the day ahead (other than for my appearance). I've got up for another wasted day, trapped in a life I wish I hadn't chosen.

Angel – let's shoot

Before I can allow myself time to self-loathe, I must prepare myself for the ultimate rat race, my London commute. The morning commute is a particular pain of living in the capital. It's a hot topic of conversation. If in the unlikely event I'm chatting with a stranger, I'll resort to asking about their journey across the city when I have little else to offer (usually pretty quickly). The commute acts as a second line of defence in this sense, behind the weather, of course. For those who are less familiar with the tube, the London Underground network is a web of 11 (soon to be 12) train lines that meander their way through over 400 kilometres of rail track beneath the city. According to the Transport for London website, there are up to 543 trains whizzing round at peak times. It's an absolute circus. It connects the city perfectly in theory; one can rarely walk for half a squared mile without passing a station. It's a perfect example of organised chaos but in the morning it is a complete nightmare.

I enter Angel station, a relatively small stop solely on the Northern Line. Entering the station is like attempting to cross the great wildebeest migration every morning; I'm like Simba caught in the gorge (apologies if it's too soon to use that as an analogy; I still hurt too). I have to perfectly time my change of direction as I zip over to the other side to swipe in. Now that contactless rules the city, swiping in merely involves flashing your card or phone over a yellow badge adjacent to the entry stalls. A few tech-savvy show-offs will use their Apple watches to swipe in, failing to realise it is less amazing and more infuriating for the masses. The yellow badge is to their right-hand side and most people wear watches on their left wrist. I thought the novelty would wear off, but it hasn't. It looks awkward. It certainly isn't impressive and should be punishable by 48-hour bans, minimum. After swiping in, I must join the bottlenecking scramble toward the escalator, which runs so deep I can feel the heat from the Earth's core towards the bottom. (Fun fact[1]: Angel station is the third deepest station in Europe). All the hard work getting ready beforehand and within eight minutes I'm covered in a glaze of my own salty sweat.

Half-awake zombies stand to the right, morning foot soldiers march on the left. Travellers can take their pick, left or right of the escalator, as long as they keep their annoying bags out of the way. To the right results in being barged into by frantic passers-by; left involves brushing every person one squeezes past when descending into the pit below. If wearing an open-collar suit, on a meeting day, also known as a day

---

1. Unsure if it is a fact, my brother told me once.

with a meeting, while clutching my laptop bag (a stereotype I am reluctant to be a part of), I am obliged to march on the left, like a Gestapo soldier, pretending I have somewhere important to be. I absolutely do not, ever. The tube is ruthless in rush hour; it is kill or be killed. I know this seems like an exaggeration but you'd be surprised how aggressive people can be. I have to make it on board or I will be left behind at the back of the queue without a thought. I'll just have to wave off the carriages that transport many others like me, who seem so desperate to get to the place that makes them feel as if they matter because they wear a suit and carry their best attempt at a stylish briefcase. Obviously, I'm different, I'm at least aware it's all a load of bollocks. I am neither one of them, nor will I ever be. By 'them' I refer to the population of generic businesspeople; the slick city folks; the cold-blooded killers of this underworld.

These blue-suit wearers are elite professionals in navigating the underground network, most likely to either the City or Canary Wharf (the real big timers are in Mayfair offices, though I'm not sure they have to worry about the tube). These delusional narcissists believe they're far more important than they actually are, just because they're on a call with a director of a FTSE 250 company at ten o'clock, cool story amigo. These maniacs bombard their way around like a maturing bull during mating season with no regard for anybody around them. They're incredibly calculated beasts, knowing the exact position of the entrance they wish to board before the train arrives. They're not afraid to check their mid-range watches furiously and sound off a 'tut' to let people know that they will be boarding the next train at any cost – alright mate, I remember my first Rolex. Personally, I give these people a wide berth when up against them. They'll find the smallest crevices to move into when boarding a train, with precisely zero care for anyone else's personal space.

Since leaving primary school, I've yet to have an arch-nemesis (I'm too much of a nice guy). The closest I've come to having one is a rather short businessman and fellow Angel commuter. The first time I came across this evil genius, he was stood at my exact spot (I have a particular tile I like to stand on), a smug smile slapped across his face knowing he was all but certain for the next train. He stood there, all five feet, negative three inches of him, punching at the keyboard of his iPhone as he responded to an impressively long list of emails (considering it was not even half past eight in the morning). Every time we cross paths, it's never me ahead of him standing there smug as I please, while he queues up behind me, letting out a huge sigh of disappointment to once again be stood behind somebody who doesn't know of his existence. One day, just one day, I'll have my vengeance.

The trains that carry us commuters around are grim; it is a journey I honestly dread every morning. I'm not sure how I've endured it at least one thousand times (I've just realised, what a depressing thought). Two thousand, if I count home too (that makes me want to cry). I stand at the platform every morning to question why I'm putting myself through this but I'm not intelligent enough to seek an answer, nor a solution. All I can do is turn toward the small, dated monitor, waiting for it to begin blinking from the far end of the platform.

TRAIN NOW APPROACHING

Journey of a lifetime

Thus begins the anticipation. Bags belonging to keen commuters rustle as they are whisked from the ground. People are desperate to jam themselves onto the approaching carriage. If they miss the train, they'll have to wait for up to two whole minutes, a short lifetime on one of the underground's platforms, especially as it means another two minutes of being on mouse watch. The curved wall opposite the platform begins to glow like an ember in the night. It is followed by a groan that builds to a crescendo from the tunnel as the train emerges from the tunnel, careering towards its next stop. By this point the crowd begins to show less regard for personal space; they shuffle their polished loafers towards the edge of the platform. The words 'Please stand behind the yellow line' painted on the floor have long been trampled over. Here we go.

The train creaks and grunts as it brakes to a gradual halt. A small crowd of roughly fifteen people (me included) scuffle as close to the doors as possible. The desperate outsiders, who have misjudged the position of the door, are scrambling their way across. Not a chance, friends. We wait. Inside the carriage, bodies press against the glass windows that have been browned after years of a lack of maintenance. The crowd is forced to quickly separate down the middle to create as narrow a passage possible for alighting commuters to fight through to earn the right to get on with their day. Two crowds are formed, each spearheaded by the veterans of the commute, the business people have been doing it for years; they know they're getting on. They're so worn by days of battle they have to wear trainers with their suits, despite looking like complete imbeciles.

I have no idea why people think wearing running trainers for the tube will improve their journey. Maybe it's to give them an advantage over us mortals (I'm lucky to wear whatever footwear I please as part of my usual working attire, as I am at meetings ten days a year, yet I've noticed no change to my journey's personal best time). Maybe it's to fool others into thinking that the trainers are actually used for running and not solely used for getting to work. After all, people love talking about their fitness regimes nowadays.

Either way, these people aren't fooling me, not a chance. The shoes are predominantly blue or grey in an attempt to match their Charles Tyrwhitt suits, with a full heel. The heel of the shoe is the giveaway, the sheer lack of erosion to the heel shows that no singular mile has been run in these shoes; they've not even done an egg and spoon race in them. They're for the purpose of getting on a train. I can't understand it myself – a training shoe for a commute? Is it too difficult to find a comfortable pair of work shoes? I'm certainly no Tom Ford, but it's distressing to witness; it makes no sense, suit and running trainers? The final kick in the teeth is when the trainers are decorated with a third colour to give them some flair; something like a lime green outlining the shoe, or a fluorescent yellow logo to give them a bit of personality – something that says 'I do what I want when I want'. Yeah, course you do, Bart Simpson. Obviously, my nemesis has blue Asics trainers with a fluorescent yellow lining on the logo. I can't help but stare each time these commute clogs catch my eye, as I know somebody is trying to give themselves an unfair advantage in the 20-inch dash. I'll shake my head as I look down, hoping someone else will be drawn to them and share in my distaste. Though I can't dwell for too long on assessing the way other people live their lives (especially from what they wear), or I miss the big commotion when the doors whoosh open. It's game on.

The entire carriage exhales and a trail of exacerbated commuters battles their way off the tube in single file. We fidget and shuffle even further, eager to board this dump of a vessel to take us on our way. I'll keep an eye on the businessman and his trainers in front, who, among the anticipation, is still calmly typing out his seventeenth email of the morning; a true professional. Then I'll see it, the gap behind the final alighting passenger beginning to emerge in front of me. Once the first move has been made (by the veteran), the floodgates open and the entire squadron hurls its bodies toward the step of the carriage. At this point, my body is acting through complete instinct. I'm on autopilot. My brain cannot think quick enough to allow me to behave rationally; I bundle and claw my way onto the tube in a shamelessly primitive manner, with no regard for any other attempting to board.

Kill or be killed.

As expected, the nemesis will slip his way onto the tube without fail every time and secure the closest space to the right of the door, turning his back on the passengers boarding so they cannot request he moves along. I envy his expertise. I'll manage to take the inside line on him or another pro, boarding to the centre of the double-doorway and landing in the middle of the carriage facing the way I'd just come from. The six-second scramble is always a blur, but nonetheless, I make it every time; standing tall, clutching the central royal-blue pole connecting floor and ceiling. I have to accept that my body is jammed every day. I'll be stood next to another sharply dressed person to my side, who will have no choice but to nobly take a light portion of my weight; something I can do nothing but be wary of. Though I'm merely 11 and a half stone, involuntarily taking any amount of dead weight can't be pleasurable.

Talking of displeasure, the worst situation I've found myself during rush hour was with a short, slight lady. My guess was she was roughly five-one, so a full foot taller than the nemesis. She'd managed to wedge her body somewhere between in front and adjacent to mine (unfortunately, this has happened more frequently than my frail mind can cope with). Her face was millimetres away from the underneath of my arm (also known as the armpit), which was outstretched over her glistening forehead as I clutched the central pole. Our bodies were so close together that she could only gaze up in the direction of my not-so-subtle double chin, which she had an outstanding view of when my head ducked towards her to dodge the many elbows that were surrounding me. For one-hundredth of a second, our eyes made contact, it felt like an eternity. I peered into her soul with a searching gaze, all I could see was sheer discomfort from the position of her body and head. I'm not even sure her feet were touching the floor. Her eyes blinked away, begging to relieve the tension – not sexual tension, not even close. It was tension caused by any sweat my body had managed to conjure since leaving my flat being pressed against the top of her head, which we were both extremely aware of.

Who's it worse for in that situation?

Once the carriage was full, we were blessed with a moment's peace, as the doors remained open. The slightly less stale air flowed in, which provided a draught and a moment for everybody to breathe. The group, once 15 strong at the doors, had been severed down to about five. Brutal. Five of us successfully boarding, that's a one-third strike rate. A solid average during rush hour. The space in the carriage was, as usual, so incredibly congested that it is impossible to move my thumb to skip the song playing on my iPhone. Tchaikovsky's 1812 overture was too dramatic for this situation, especially as I was scared people would be able to hear it (I tend to kid myself that listening to classical music makes me somehow cool – a fool more like). The bodies on the train in rush hour behave like particles in a solid state. As the tiny space is so compact, it's as if they are one. The lady and my armpit were most certainly one. The gentle hum from beneath the vehicle (and the quiet tunes of Tchaikovsky) was the only sound that broke through the silence, until, "Can you move down please?" The rush hour classic.

Though I couldn't see who asked, this usually comes from an unsuccessful business boarder with a bruised ego, expecting 20 people jam-packed into a space the size of a phone box to mix and shuffle about like a game of Tetris to allow them to board. You just wait there. There is absolutely no way these people can wait up to two whole minutes for the next train to arrive. I tried not to, but couldn't help a good old-fashioned eye roll and low-key tut, too fatigued by the previous 30 seconds (basically too scared) to tell them to piss off and wait like everybody else.

"Please stand clear of the closing doors," came from the heavens. At last, I was on.

It is only as the train hurtles towards the next station I can once again think clearly. I begin to accustom myself to the discomfort, almost embracing it. Surely this is better than driving through rush hour traffic? I don't have to concentrate on foot pedals or the traffic ahead, no checking my rear view or side mirrors. I can surrender myself to the current and let myself be taken down the Thames courtesy of Transport For London.

Once I began to settle down on my very own Groundhog Day, I motioned around the tube with my eyes, engaging in some people-watching to pass the time and to reassure the lady, who was inhaling my armpit, to not be intimidated. Not that I am intimidating in any way; I've got too much of a baby face, even if I don't shave for a week. I only grow six hairs on my chin. She would be reassured that I, unlike other creepy commuters, wouldn't just stare at her from above. I was far too tired to be convincing myself that a woman who simply made eye contact with me does in fact want to mother my children. I always make a conscious effort to not stare at anybody, but I'm convinced some primitive instinct inside us still has the ability to override rational thinking; curiosity takes over. It could be anything: a birthmark, a scar, a pretty face (male or female, I don't discriminate). We sometimes have to take a swift look, just in case.

My eyes continued to work their way around the carriage from person to person, each keeping their heads down, staring at the ground blankly, headphones in, glum faces. It was like a strange alternate version of the opening scene of *Saving Private Ryan*. Of course, we weren't on our way to all but certain death, but we were crammed into a vessel, with our heads down, in total silence. Maybe that's not my best analogy. This time of day is a glum atmosphere (if you hadn't guessed), made worse for me by the feeling that not only am I in close contact with other people's sweat, or their morning breath, but I am festering among their germs. Unfortunately, there are no hygiene requirements to board the tube. I suppose it wouldn't be fair, but when I'm in such close proximity to somebody that I can taste how much hairspray they've applied, or I can see the facial hair they've missed in their rushed shave earlier this morning, I can't help but wish for a screening process. The tube is a mini germ underworld. I'll often experience moments of panic through fear I may catch a cold, impetigo, or worse as my senses begin to register with my brain again, after the out-of-body experience when boarding.

The poles we have to clutch are warm and damp as if they have been dipped in a giant tub of petroleum jelly. I can feel the lack of hand washing from the body temperature moisture that covers the pole like a glaze. I recall the stench of stale coffee on the breath of the man taking my weight that morning, (I'm a gambling man and I'd gamble on him being a software developer going off the pen in his shirt breast pocket) combined with the view of his jacket lapel that was lightly powdered with flakes of dandruff that were no more than six inches from my face. I could do nothing but hold my breath and tilt my head backward. There was a slight jerk of the train and the man taking my weight was thrust into me, or at least his flake-filled lapel was. As I was unable to bleach my face instantly, the porridge that was sitting in my stomach began to toy with the idea of reappearing; I quickly felt the back of my head dampening with sweat more than usual and my throat tightening. My mouth began to salivate, *I can not throw up here,* I thought, gazing once again at the forehead of the unfortunate damsel next to me, which would be the centre of the projection zone. Bullseye.

I exhaled through my mouth, blowing towards the ceiling, frantically trying to compose myself. The blackness from outside the carriage turned to light as we arrived at Old Street station. Again the shuffling began and I could feel space begin to appear behind me. I begged my body, *Please hold on.* The doors whooshed open and even the stale air of the underground felt pure, as it rushed in. It was slightly cooler than the air inside the carriage, but 'slightly' was more than enough for my body to calm down. I had to swallow the puddle of saliva that had collected in my mouth, as I had nowhere to spit. The warm bile bounced inside my stomach, making me burp (I only ever burp when I throw up). I clenched my lips together as I felt my breakfast soar through my chest and up to the back of my mouth. I swallowed sharply (definitely a terrible idea) and my chest began to burn. I clenched my lips and began to breathe rapidly through a tiny hole in my mouth; I must have looked like I was going into labour. I forced myself to continue to stare into the blinding lights on the ceiling. I heard the doors close and realised I'd missed the entire station scuffle in my moment of madness. To think I was moments away from producing my own Jackson Pollock potentially on another human's head. I looked down to realise the carriage had lost a significant portion of the horde, which allowed me room to bend over slightly and catch my breath. I clutched the same slimy pole as before and stared down into the light reflecting off the floor. I knew I wouldn't be sick on anybody's forehead. Panic over. I would live to cry another day.

Mercifully, the carriage loses about a third of its passengers at Old Street station, the Shoreditch stop in east-central London. Shoreditch has become the fresh hub for start-up businesses, the kind of workplaces to have foosball tables in their office and that go on team retreats to Thailand for ten days of bonding/bondage. Filled with the kind of companies that encourage employees to bring their whole self to the office instead of masking their personality with a corporate visage. I find it admirable yet I am apprehensive of the idea at the same time (not sure I'll ever trust people I work with, especially in London). Friday afternoons aren't really part of the working week for the Shoreditch community; drinks start any time from lunchtime, especially in the summer, where the rooftop bars are swamped by bookings from all the edgy businesses. The Queen of Hoxton is always a goldmine on a Friday in summer, filled with ambitious young professionals (who identify as yo-pros) who've commuted from Clapham and Brixton and are desperate to be part of the next Facebook or Google. If one is ever searching for a discussion on next-generation data analytics or marketing techniques, this is the place to find every sales team and account manager. I'm sure it's really interesting over a drink nonetheless. These companies partially dictate how we think after all (remind me to take off my tinfoil hat).

As the tube doors close on Old Street station, I finally have space to manoeuvre. My shamelessly branded bag no longer has to be wedged between my knees. I can hold it at my side, on show for everyone to be super-impressed (of course, I didn't buy it myself, I'm on a pitiful graduate salary). At this point, I'm grateful to have adequate room to stand freely and not have germy members of the public touching me. I'm aware I'm as germy as any of them, thank you.

Once I leave Old Street aboard a train that doesn't involve

me getting skin flakes in my mouth or having other people's faces pressed against me leaving imprints of their make-up, I can relax with my thoughts; my mind is free at last. It is then I allow myself to switch off and enjoy the ride, or at least I tell myself that. How wrong I am. I hate being alone with my thoughts. My extensive sense of self-awareness makes me my own worst enemy. Pondering over and over inside my own head about a conversation I may have had six weeks ago, or the time my shorts were pulled down in PE during my first year of senior school, in front of the girl I fancied, Kathryn, for her to see my baby-penis. She confirmed it on MSN Messenger later that evening. Gutted. It is so cruel being scarred with memories as such; they randomly appear in my mind without warning. It's as if once I have zero distractions, my brain chooses to delve into my library of horrific memories from the last 24 years, to make me feel even worse. Imagine our brains anticipating that; while we are feeling apprehensive about going to work, mulling over the day's uncertainty, they decide to completely throw us off guard with a curve ball to amplify any negative feelings. Cheers for that. Just as I stand and begin to compose myself for the working day, headphones in with a relaxing orchestral piece playing, my mind will hit me again, what next, the time I scratched my auntie's new car? Admittedly it was a horrific experience and would be for any nine-year-old.

Obviously, I didn't mean it. I was only nine. I was short as a child and was always desperate to be taller. Though my cousin was a year younger, he was much taller than I was. I was too short for his bike. I knew I was too short to comfortably control it, yet I begged him to let me ride it through his street. I used to adore riding a bike (until I started driving, now riding a bike reminds me of those ignorant cyclists who think the world owes them something). The wind blasting in my face as I travelled at speeds I imagined weren't even possible. The freedom of riding past the end of the road, out of view from any parents or authority, I became free because of my bike. Riding a bike brought such joy to me as a child, until this wretched day. I was dashing around the bottom of my cousin's road having the time of my life. I was perched so high from the ground on this Goliath of a bike. It felt like a motorbike, but faster. I looked back at the stretch of tarmac; it was a runway and I was a fighter pilot preparing for take-off. My legs were the engines, ready to let loose. I took a second to receive the all-clear for take-off, when suddenly, halfway down the runway, my cousin appeared and began motioning for us to go inside. We'd been called in for tea (evening meal, call it what you want).

He hopped inside and I rushed back towards his house to follow him. Just as I pulled in parallel to my auntie's new car on the driveway I squeezed both brakes with each of my middle fingers (they were the only fingers that could reach the brakes), but I lost control of the enormous bike and veered to my left, towards the car. The edge of the left handlebar met the back right-hand door of the car at the most acute of angles. I pushed with every shred of force I could muster in my left leg to steer away from the car, but my legs were too short. My toe could only brush the floor and the bike fell to the left. I jolted forward, as did the bike. I shoved myself off the car to stop my face colliding with the window, overturning the bike to its right, which threw my four-foot short self to the floor.

My knee ignited with pain from the deep graze I'd earned in the fall. A true battle wound in childhood. The pain was excruciating, it burned my entire right knee, but I could not cry; men didn't cry (though I've found this to be a complete lie). My lip trembled, my tear ducts filled with water. I was desperate to release my tears, but no. I swallowed hard and wiped my eyes before turning to the bike to pick it u- oh no. A jagged white scratch, imitating a lightning bolt, roughly one metre long, had torn across both doors on the right-hand side of the car. I didn't know any swear words at the time, but that would have been the perfect time to use one. I felt sick from the dread, *I'll be in so much trouble. Auntie will have to buy another new car. My mum and dad will kill me. What do I do?* The longer I stared, the larger the scratch became. It wasn't only the length but the impressive depth too. What would I do?

I was forced to act as any innocent child does. I skipped inside, ready to enjoy my chicken dippers, smiley faces and beans – a true staple in my childhood diet. I remember being sat at the table, thinking of how I'd pretend to be stunned when I saw the scratch for the first time, or so my auntie and cousin would think. For all they knew I'd cycled an extra lap on the bike. Foolproof. However, when my auntie saw the scratch for the first time and being an adult able to add two plus two to make four, she knew it was one of us. It was almost as if the scratch began at a similar height to the handlebars of the bike.

My eyes welled up as she asked me, calmy, "Andrew, do you know what happened to my car?"

Even when reminiscing, I gulp hard to hold back the tears of nine-year-old me, 15 years later and taking the tube to work. I have to clear my throat thinking about that day.

I didn't purposely scratch the car, but I did go on the bike after being told it was too big for me. Was it really my fault? I wished desperately for the situation to end. I wish this memory and so many others would fade away and not haunt me. But, as the scratch didn't fade, this vivid flashback won't. I didn't even have to tell my auntie what happened, she knew, family always does. Bursting into tears was the giveaway. Guilty as charged. However, it got much worse as my auntie said the words no child wants to hear when out with their companions.

"I'm calling your mum."

I didn't want to go to jail. I didn't want to be told I couldn't play football. I didn't want to be in any trouble. I was too innocent. I still am too innocent. If only I could help myself from being tormented by this living nightmare of a flashback. Onlookers boarding the tube must surely be baffled seeing me as I am being choked by a deep thought from my own past. All I seek in the morning is a clear head for work yet there I am silently pleading my own innocence from scratching my auntie's car in 2003. Pathetic then. Pathetic now.

"We are now approaching London Bridge," says a voice from above.

Time to refocus; time to change. London Bridge, one of the central stations in London; it's always rammed. It sits beneath The Shard, which is just over 1,000 feet tall. The 95-storey building is the true centrepiece of the London skyline. Its pristine glass shell is worthy of standing among Manhattan's finest buildings as if it were one of the shorter, (and of course) leaner English cousins to the Freedom Tower, One World Trade Center.

Being in the shadow of The Shard every morning gives me the London buzz, I feel excited knowing I'm in one of the world's biggest cities until I see the crowd of people I've got to wade through in London Bridge station, time and time again. As the doors screech open, I grip my bag tightly, shoving it in front of my body to use as a blast shield. I was once attempting to make an exit when I was bombarded by a two-strap trooper, the most annoying of all commuters. The two-strap trooper is a male (only ever male) who wears an annoyingly large backpack, with both straps over his shoulders. The straps are tightly fastened so he and the bag move as one body. I believe these people were the children in school who would run everywhere hunched over, facing downwards, with their clenched fists reaching behind them towards the sky. They're now just ignorant people and continue to pester in adult life, as they tense every muscle in their body to march around, causing innocent passers-by to bounce off them as they smash their way through the crowd like a freight train in the night at full pelt. It's too early for my body to experience such force, so I tend to steer clear. That is having learned to steer clear after thinking I'd cunningly snaked my way around one on Groundhog Day 472. (I can't guarantee it was actually my 472nd day, sorry.) However, I couldn't escape the girth of his backpack. My body bounced off the backpack into the direction of (no doubt) an incredibly important businesswoman. I managed to drive my toe into the floor to prevent smashing into her, which took plenty of effort for morning me. Her reactive "tut" notified me that she was displeased that I'd delayed her by one and a half seconds. How ignorant of me.

I must wind my way through a crowd that is six rows deep and stretches across the entire platform. My movement emulates the early versions of the 90's game Snake. I move so rigidly it's painful (almost impressive) how long it takes to move ten feet away from a train. I endure this every working day. Usually, by the time I've battled through, I get so paranoid about being mugged I have to have a full pocket touch-down to ensure nothing's missing; I'm sure that day will come. As I walk through, worming my way across the station knowing I'm beneath one of the country's most impressive skyscrapers, I'll try to contemplate big city life, wondering if this is what I envisaged in my teens before actually moving here. I contemplate whether life would be any different in New York. I long to live there as I once longed to live in London, but I will always lose the desire to live there by asking myself, *can I cope with their freedom?*

I marvel at how much Americans enjoy the word 'freedom', and what freedom actually means. Monuments, the national anthem, even in music (Pharrell Williams' song 'Freedom' is a banger though); they bloody adore the notion of freedom. Perhaps it is a concept that is alien to me; as I haven't witnessed my ancestors fight for their own (give or take learning about a couple of world wars in school). The word liberty seems to arouse a significant portion of their population. Fully grown men walking round with daylong erections, which they have to seat-belt in their trousers every 4th July as they repeatedly chant "Freedom!" There is an American way of shouting the word 'Freedom'. I've experienced one Independence Day while in (supposedly liberal) California and it was all a bit much for me. They're like the far right on steroids across the Atlantic. It is as if the Brexit mob took inspiration from the American ways of living. Perhaps the next British general election candidates will promise to host a referendum on the legalisation of gun ownership. I'm sure the mob would be all over that one. It'd be like another nationwide mid-life crisis, fully grown adults campaigning for guns to protect our properties and take back control. I daren't even think about that happening. British people with guns, you'd have shootings in the local Greggs' cafes over the last chicken bake, turf wars at Cornwall, and weekly assassination attempts at West Ham United's football stadium; the country would be in utter chaos. It's feasible that New York would be safer than London in that case; they do have strict gun laws. By strict, I refer to the fact that in 2019, I could be killed with a shotgun or a rifle, but if somebody would prefer to take aim at me with a pistol, they must have a licence; that's understandable. That's safe.

In any walk of life, the curiosity in one's mind dictates, it's whether the curiosity is powerful enough to make us act, or we spend our lives wishing for something else. If I live in New York, I'd be among the most beautiful man-made skyline in the world. I'd be well connected along the East Coast of the

US. I'd be able to nibble away at my lunch in Central Park every day. But alternatively, I may fly there and be shot dead by a legally owned weapon within a couple of weeks, to that I must say, "no thank you." I wouldn't say fear of death puts me off living there, but for me living somewhere is preferable to being dead somewhere else. That's probably a convincing reason to remain.

It's impressive how, when deep in thought, your memory function disables and you have no idea of what's been occurring around you. There I was walking through a train station when I began thinking about New York and suddenly my attention is abruptly drawn to Ludovico Einaudi's 'Primavera' playing through my headphones. I find myself aboard a reasonably empty eastbound Jubilee line train with no idea of how I made it here. The only advantage of work beginning at half past nine is that the second train requires no struggle so we can move on at last. Next stop, Canary Wharf. It's time.

(If you thought I dragged this chapter out, its average reading time matches my average commute. Painful, isn't it?)

Chapter II – What am I doing here?

Dwarf in the wharf

Media, through its many forms, warps our perception of places around the world. In my teens, I was always driven by the prospect of working in Canary Wharf and have been ever since watching Rowan Atkinson as Johnny English. I was inspired in particular by the scene where he parachutes into Canary Wharf as part of his stealth stalking of the evil villain Pascal Sauvage. This was the first time I felt in awe of London and knew that it was where I wanted to be – what a beautiful skyline.

If we're talking about penis size, of course size doesn't matter; at least that's what most of us think. Not much else I can say, really. It's not about the size of the wave; it's all about the motion in the ocean. But when it comes to the building you work in, size matters. I wanted to be the man who strolled in and took the lift up to floor 40-something, or even 50. I didn't want to settle for just London; I knew I wanted to work in Canary Wharf. I was drawn to the tall buildings built for enormous companies to exert their global influence. It's what I've wanted since I realised I couldn't make a living from being a footballer. Again, I'm not bitter (part of me is still hoping this will somehow happen). I don't dream about scoring in front of the fans and jumping into the crowd, then emerging from the riot to bow before them and shuffle back to the halfway line. That doesn't matter to me anymore. I don't lie in bed thinking I'm a failure, why would I?

(I'll try to stop mentioning it.)

When I received my offer to work for a firm in Canary Wharf, I felt for once in my life, I'd finally succeeded in myself. After disappointing exam results (for my parents especially) compared to my 'ability' throughout school and university, I somehow pulled a top training contract out of the bag. I was one of those 'he could have gone to Oxford if he'd have put the effort in' bods. Okay Mum, chill out it was seven years ago; we've been through this. (Definitely couldn't have by the way.) After never-ending applications for graduate schemes and countless rejections – most of whom didn't even respond – I somehow blagged myself through a five-stage application process and landed a job in Canary Wharf. *Here we go*, I'd tell myself, *Big leagues, big bucks, this is it, Drew*. I was going to make it. That is until I saw the building I would be working in. My building, of course, is one of the stumps. Out of shame, I must opt for the internal route to the office, through Canary Wharf shopping centre, too embarrassed to enter the stubby 12-floor box that cowers in the shadow of One Canada Square (the tallest building; it has the pyramid on top). For many, the walk to work is a mundane task that requires little brain energy. I pass thousands of vacant faces on the walk to work, seemingly content with the journey they are on, both there and in life.

Why aren't I?

Before I even step off the tube and onto the platform, the work dread will begin tormenting me. Out of the fire. *Oh no, how many emails will I have? Will I leave on time this evening? Will I have to have any conversations with people I feel awkward talking to?* I can't simply focus on getting from the underground (dump) to the lower ground level of Canary Wharf shopping centre swarmed by a sea of briefcases, shiny shoes and DJ headphones connected wirelessly to the latest smart phones (tech-savvy people – no wires anymore).

Citibank, Barclays, J.P. Morgan, Morgan Stanley, all the finance heavyweights are here; it is the lion's den, if the lion was scrawny, worn from the stress of its day job and took its moods out on everybody else. My slender build can navigate quickly across the platform to the long stretch of corridor leading to the office I apply my monotonous trade. Once I'm through the glass double doors connecting the tube station to the shopping centre, I'm on my way – oh no, wait. The floor is tiled.

Being obsessed with the number four (for absolutely no reason), I must walk counting my paces in sets of four. People have their own number, three, five, maybe even six, (why I have no idea). Four is a square number, four is an even number, four is a pure number. Why wouldn't I want to live life through the number four? You may believe there are more important happenings in life than standing on a crack with your left foot, however, my brain doesn't. It's like having a mental block. The tiles beneath my feet are slightly too short for one tile to match my stride length, but too long for two tiles to compensate. I must make my way to work, through the art of dance.

I, like most white men, cannot dance. I'm unsure why this is; possibly our joints are made of wood, but we're so rigid when we try to move our hips to a beat. A dance floor full of white men is a rotten affair, clicking fingers and biting lips to the dropping of a beat; it needs to stop. Can we all stop? The dancing is even more disastrous when we're drunk and a classic begins to play; one of those songs that when we hear, we point our index finger to the skies uncontrollably thinking, 'This is our shit! I love you!' Something like 'Mr Brightside' by The Killers, 'Country Roads' by John Denver, or any catchy tune that you pretend to loathe until it comes on while you're drunk (I won't even entertain the idea of people dancing along to 'Come on Eileen'. I actually hate that song).

We are, for reasons unknown, possessed by this music when intoxicated. When we hear the chorus to a catchy melody our bodies surge into action. We tilt our heads back, open our arms with hands reaching as far as we can. As the chorus kicks in, we pogo before our fellow chums, who are equally as pitiful. Abhorrent. I am reminded of my woeful dancing ability every morning, as I have to make my way across the walkway of hell to the stumpy building's entrance with my two left feet. My stride length increases in an attempt to avoid all cracks where the tiles connect. *One, two, three, four, one, two, three, four,* I recite in my head as I storm across the glossy cream tiles. It's almost too easy to begin with; child's play. I'm cruising along with my head above the clouds until I reach my first step, one short of completing my second round of four fours. The maniac behind the floor's design decided to have a blue semi-circular line cutting across the middle of this floor to let people know they've arrived at the atrium of the shopping centre. Not that the enormous glass dome above would give anything away. Who would do that? Perhaps he was a number-five man with smaller legs and knew it would fall on step 40. Surely his stride length isn't as impressive as mine. I'd be like a gazelle darting through the African savannah, like Concorde zipping through the air, but for this fool's design.

I've had to make a routine for a walk to work based on floor tiles; taking the same line every day. Why me? My body refuses to deviate off path for fear of looking like I am actually trying to Greek dance step my way to work and I'll be forced to plant my right foot onto the navy tile on step 32. I am then bound to the blue semi-circle for at least four steps on each foot, crack depending. I'm forced to dodge my way past suitcases, tote bags, two strapped backpacks, Asics trainers; it quickly becomes a minefield in the centre of the shopping atrium. *Six, seven, eight!* I have to reach with my right foot to stay on track for the semi-circle, but that's allowed, my world, my rules. At the edge of the blue tightrope, the floor is no longer lava; I've made it through.

Sometimes, I get so preoccupied I forget to hold my breath as I pass the world's worst-smelling supermarket (no prizes for guessing the supermarket in Canary Wharf is a massive Waitrose). As is common practice in the capital, supermarket shelves are disproportionately stacked with sushi (and avocados). This particular supermarket even has a sushi counter, so people can enjoy super-raw fish. But this is situated directly in front of the air conditioning unit, which stinks out the atrium directly outside. The only thing worse than the smell of this supermarket is not hitting my fours. I've got to hit me them fours.

I probably look like a circus clown, walking an imaginary navy tight rope, but the world doesn't pay me that level of attention; I don't think so anyway. I can put an end to the anxious feelings from stepping across a shopping centre and continue with the worries of work. The doom and gloom of heading into a world I have zero fulfilment from. Heading towards a grey desk with three computer screens that I will sit behind for at least ten miserable hours of an uninspiring day, analysing the amount of money others make, on work that I (and those around me) slave away for. Is this the job I desired? Why am I walking into this? I'm not making a positive impact on society, or doing something that fills me with joy; I don't love being here. Surely I can't spend my life analysing financial information. My constant act of pretending to be interested in a company's profit and loss account drains me, as I lie through my teeth, regularly claiming that a company's revenue drivers in financial year ending 2019 are 'so interesting'. It's like solving a Rubik's cube to survive, but every square on the surface is grey and every move goes unnoticed unless it's somehow wrong. People will say, "that's life," or "it's part of growing up", but why? Every day I ascend the stairs into the building I'll ask myself, *does this have to be it?*

Getting into character

My greatest struggle with working in London's financial sector is the notion of bringing my whole self to work (I can't enter the office telling everyone I don't want to be here). This is where I admit I secretly envy the Shoreditch cool kids alighting at Old Street station. Being in my twenties, human and having limited interest in the *Financial Times*, I find it difficult to naturally be enthusiastic in the workplace. Therefore, I must perform another act – my professional self.

My professional self can be turned on with the flick of a switch as I enter the stumpy office building, reluctantly getting into character. My professional self is the cheerful, all smiles and relaxed colleague who's extroverted in nature and keeps the floor as happy as he is. He even does four o'clock chocolate runs to the smelly supermarket downstairs (despite being one of the lowest paid). My professional self is interested in the world of mergers and acquisitions and is able to perform extensive amounts of financial analysis in a short time frame, making other people's lives easier. He's the perfect cover. My professional self, however, cannot stop me from not wanting to talk to anybody in the morning. I try to keep my head down all the way to my desk. This is my first challenge in work; find a route to my desk without having to engage in meaningless conversation that neither party is interested in. This is not because I'm impolite, but to save others, and me, from a wholly false exchange, which neither of us remembers by the time I take my first (of many) coffee breaks.

I enter the lobby. The enormous open space is impressive the first time you lay eyes on her (I prefer to say 'it' rather than 'her', but 'her' seems cool to say, which clearly I am not). A magnificent reception desk stands to the left of 20 slick glass gates, which lead to the lifts and a viewing point that goes all the way up to the roof of the building. Three immaculate faces, masters in the art of client schmoozing, guard the guest entrances to the far right toward the conference rooms at the back. The conference rooms are out of view due to the grand marble staircase that leads you to the first floor – the client floor – which is more like the lobby of a chic five-star hotel than an office building. Corporate logos and slogans are at every turn: plastered on the walls, slapped over the lift doors, even the corporate motto wraps around the lanyard of every ID badge to remind us of who we represent. Every firm is the same. Corporate spiel is shoved down the throats of employees to make us feel like we are part of a bigger picture and that we matter, but we all know in reality that we aren't (bonuses remind me that I'm particularly unimportant). The firms will always live on, with or without us. I have a particular distaste towards being force-fed marketing bollocks. Nobody goes to work with the thought of 'I want to be as honest in my communication as possible today' (definitely not in this line of work), or 'I can't wait to provide meaningful insights to my clients'. Anyone who does is either a liar or a partner. Partners (directors, executives, bosses) are paid handsomely enough to be happy to do so.

I usually time my song choice for entering the office, something that is capable of motivating me to have a positive attitude and overcome the feeling of wasting my life by being here. I like an inspiring orchestral piece to gear my professional self up for another performance in the art of deception. A fitting choice, Hans Zimmer's 'Now We Are Free' as I prepare for another day of enslaving myself, nothing gladiatorial about it. Somehow it makes me feel like I'll attack the day ahead. If Maximus can make it through the fighting pits as a slave, I can get through this. I'm not a musical person, I long to be, but I could not even get past Grade 1 guitar. Listening to music can change any mood, you just need the right song. Listening to an orchestra makes my chest rise, my shoulders ease back and my head lift from its drooped position. I no longer have the posture of a vulture. I'm striding with purpose. I matter, my work matters, I feel unstoppable, for now.

The only thing to stop me in my tracks is crossing paths with a colleague I vaguely know. Much like Lee Gi (Gi pronounced 'Jee' – for the avoidance of doubt, all names are fake, sorry). I'll be transformed by the music, finding the similarities in my struggle with that of everybody's favourite gladiator when out the corner of my eye, I see him. He's simply a short fellow who was in another college class to mine during our first year, when we had to pass 14 exams to not be asked to leave the firm. We all have a handful of Lee Gis in our lives, the kind of individual that we seldom see but for an occasion such as, in our case, the end of exams. I've found work events and weddings are the prime occasions for such interaction. Occasions whereby we pretend not to see our opposite number until after we've each had a hearty amount of alcohol and thus begin to make the mistake of gravitating toward one other. We finally say hello and proceed to stand at a bar for anything up to an hour, discussing how we should plan meeting up for a drink every month or so, or that we should elope to Ibiza together. Of course, the following morning we wake up and nervously check our phones as we pretend the conversation didn't happen. We are desperate to forget the words that left our mouths. We can only hope we never get the morning-after text, asking when we're going for that drink, for then it really gets complicated.

Lee Gi and I would have these conversations every time we finished exams in the class year of 2017. Every six to eight weeks, we'd catch up on the same spiel. By the end we'd just recite the conversation. I was happy to see him for ten minutes and not a second longer. He no doubt thought the same about me. We'd nod to each other if we caught eyes on the way to our separate classrooms in the real world (there were four classes on the same intake) and save our conversation until we were slurring our words and wouldn't remember exactly what was said. I'd wake with a gut feeling our conversation got deeper than I intended. Strange how I'd trust somebody I barely knew but had a total understanding with. After our 14th exam I wasn't sure where Lee Gi and I would head, but I didn't feel the need to ask. We chatted, went our separate ways and ceased seeing one another. Then one morning (having not seen him for the best part of a year) there he was, three people in front of me in the morning lift queue.

I began planning my getaway route. I couldn't be bothered taking my headphones out and having a conversation. I decided I'd pretend I was going to the gym on the basement floor and allow people in front of me before I could make the quick switch back into the lifts heading to the tenth floor. This is the ability to think quickly and solve problems that firms look for when interviewing candidates. Surely this plan would work. I looked around to see the queue behind me; it was long enough to fill eight lifts. I could easily snake my way into another lift at the price of being delayed by one minute. I turned back around to check for progress in front to see Lee Gi staring back at me. There was no escape now.

The moment we made eye contact my gladiatorial power drained from me. The music wooing my mind vanished and the voice in my head began prepping questions to ask and be asked. I became anxious like walking into an interview. *Do I have to? It's still too early for a lift natter.* That's me conversing with myself in my head. Lift natters are among the most difficult conversations one can have at work, especially when you've got a lift-full of witnesses who don't want to hear a conversation you don't want to have. There is no escape, trapped in a box with strangers for much longer than you're comfortable with. My foremost fear is, without doubt, does my breath smell? I (as we all do) will aim my mouth away from people I'm talking to as a common courtesy; nobody likes inhaling stale toothpaste masking the scent of morning coffee with a hint of banana. Throw in a dash of bullshit too. I obsess over my own dental care, but a 40-minute commute to work in an underground furnace dries my mouth out. It needs dusting and a litre of water before I can talk to anybody. I have been on the end of some pungent conversations; the kind where you force out a smile while wincing at the waft of bad breath, as you counteract with a powerful nasal exhale. We've all been there.

I raised my hand to cup my nose and breathed out of my mouth, immediately followed by a sharp inhale through the nose in an attempt to detect any bad smell. I usually pretend I'm scratching my nose to not give the game away. Stale toothpaste and coffee (no banana), could be worse and definitely could be better.

A green light above the fifth and final lift, on the right-hand side of the corridor branching off from the office's main atrium, began to flash. The winding queue of zombies shuffled its way down to the far lift. The words, 'Reaching new heights for our clients' beamed across the lift doors atop of a birds-eye view shot of a skydiver perched above a stunning coastline. How inspiring. I knew where I'd rather be (though I'm not sure that's necessarily true, we'll come to that much later). If only my eyes could be spared the marketing slogans. The doors eased open and the coastline view of white sand meeting sapphire water disappeared, replaced by a void, a dim grey chamber. I felt my head sink to the floor as the single-file train entered the void to its capacity. I feel like a lamb with a rope round its neck being led to slaughter when I go through this motion, why do I even bother being here? True hardship, I know; embarrassingly ignorant of the fortune I've had to land this job, especially with a Lower Second-Class Honours degree, a modern-day miracle (also known as privilege/'extenuating circumstances').

Why me?

I stared through my shoes while each plodded in front of the other, avoiding the cracks on the floor without my navigation (after 24 years of militant training). All I feel in this place is disappointment and emptiness, like I'm offering nothing to the world (I have to force myself to not drag my heels, like when I was going for a haircut as a child and too scared because I hated the sounds of the clippers around my ears. I hated it). I'd completely zoned out by the time I crossed the boundary between lobby and lift. I looked up and there he was, Lee Gi. He'd been there all along, eyes fixated on me, cracking a nervous smile. We must remember that Lee Gi is thinking the same as we are; he doesn't want this either. He doesn't need to know about my meaningless life; he just wants to get through his own day (not as exciting as mine, obviously). No chance he'd care or find out I've said that. Knowing this, I relaxed at first, pushing my bottom lip upwards into my thinned top lip and raising my eyebrows (to add more wrinkles to my forehead) in an effort to muster a smile. I removed my (non-DJ) headphones.

"Hi, how're you doing?"

It rolls off my tongue having been here for three years. The same four words, every time. Before I gave him time to reply, I turned around and reached through bodies for the unlit '10' button. As I pulled away from the panel and turned to him, Lee Gi let out a sigh.

"Not too bad thanks, how about you?"

I paused for a second, let my eyes wander, and asked myself one more time, *why am I here?*

It could have been the morning after his mother's funeral, or the day before his wedding and I'd have received exactly the same response. I wanted to scream, but couldn't. I had to control my emotions, especially as it wasn't even half past nine. People don't need screaming at that time, especially not with stale toothpaste, coffee and now a thick aroma of bullshit making up part of the attack. The lift warmed up quickly with bodies crammed in shoulder to shoulder. I knew I had to respond to Lee Gi, who was pretending to seem interested in me, playing his part impeccably in this hopeless charade.

"Yeah I'm alright, just a bit tired this morning."

What else could I say? At least there was a shred of truth in my response. I'm shattered every morning, though I couldn't tell him about my double life –being caught with another woman thus getting little sleep – before enduring a hellish journey to a place I can't bear. I'm shattered by life, Lee Gi (he really didn't need to know because we all are). The last time Lee Gi and I saw each other we were moaning about how we don't spend enough time together (I detest anything that comes out of my mouth after more than two drinks). This was our chance, wasn't it? There we were, nowhere else to go, we must be able to offer each other a lifeline for the day. I toyed with the idea of saying 'Let's go for a coffee this morning, I'll send you an invite'. Invites are always essential as they block out your diary showing others you are busy. Being weirdly nervous I hesitated. I have no idea why. I was at a loss what to say. I devolved into my 15-year-old self with bushy hair and a dental brace trying to strike up a conversation with a girl. It was almost as if I had feelings for Lee Gi.

That's not me, I don't think.

He swallowed hard and broke the silence with, "Have you

been busy recently?"

Come on, I didn't deserve that. Any feelings of empathy for Lee Gi died when he asked his follow-up question. It's a box-ticking question from chapter one, page one in the guide to numbing somebody's brain in the hope you bore them to death and beyond. Next up are the weather and the commute (thanks for reading).

Go away, Lee Gi.

What a vacuous question to continue this hollow conversation. It's a question for a chirpy cab driver out of politeness, not me. With cab drivers the point is to set them off on a 20-minute tale about the recent decision to become a taxi driver (always recent and part time) to fill the days, to give them something to do, while I tap away at my phone and say 'Yeah' every 30 seconds. You know the kind, 'I was a lower league footballer but have retired and bought a few properties'. Now they need something to do, so have decided to do a few hours a week chauffeuring people around the city. Their stories are always obscure enough that I can't tell whether they're telling a lie. The fact that I ask this question through faux politeness and sheer ignorance is why I dislike people asking me if I am or have been busy. Maybe I should start responding by telling them I could have been a professional footballer (sorry, I did say I'll stop).

(Definitely could have if I was good enough.)

As a graduate, we have no control over how quiet or hectic the days are; we are at the beck and call of anyone and everyone at the firm we work for. Of course, we're busy. If we aren't busy then we're handed tasks to busy ourselves; they call it 'business development'. Business Development (BD for short, classic) translates as, 'We don't have anything meaningful for you to do, because you are meaningless'. I'll be asked to spend a day of my life producing analysis on the correlation of bee population decline in the UK with

Facebook's share price on the NASDAQ. I am deeply grateful for any opportunity and repeat 'Yes, of course' submissively, about 13 times to convey how enthusiastic I am for the work. Though inside I know this is to keep me busy while the adults work. I feel pathetic to the point it cripples my posture. This is being busy, this is the life that I've allowed myself to sell out to; my backbone is not strong enough for me to walk away. Lee Gi doesn't want to know any of this, he only wants my cooperation in the façade and all I want is this lift to get to the tenth floor. The lift doors slid open to interrupt my thought. I turned to see what floor we were on, my time to make an exit, please? Floor five, only halfway.

Our silence was broken by a series of over-polite 'excuse me' and 'thank you' exchanges as room freed up for me to face Lee Gi.

"Have I been busy?" I repeated the question and zoned back in. "Yeah slightly, no late nights recently so I can't complain. I'm on a fairly interesting project at the minute so I'm stuck in a project room without windows. I would say I'm missing the sunlight but we don't get any."

Fantastic performance. I'm a born liar, zero truth behind it, even a joke about the weather. Get in. I awaited the forced laugh and his response knowing I've played my part. Floor ten needed to hurry up, we were dying in that lift.

He grinned and forced his work laugh through a smile (I hope he didn't believe that was my idea of humour). I pretend to not care what people think to pave over abysmal weather references I make for a cheap laugh in times of need. I just want to be accepted, though I can't admit it to people.

He replied unprompted, "Yeah it's not been great recently, I've been pulling a few late ones, was in until midnight last night finalising a report for whopper that we've been working on for seven weeks."

It felt odd, I couldn't recall probing him for a response.

This does happen a lot in work, therefore I'm accustomed to receiving unwanted information as such. I still can't believe he used the word 'whopper' without being ironic. "Midnight is a killer," I responded, with no other follow-up enquiries from my end.

He let out a long exhale (away from my nose thankfully) coming back with a "Yeah." Nothing else. Offering nothing, but half a grin out the side of his mouth and a desperate look in his eyes. He couldn't say anything else. He didn't need to.

"Yeah."

I killed the conversation, we both nodded and our eyes wandered as the lift came to a halt at floor ten. Finally.

"This is me anyway, good to see you, mate, all the best." I didn't even allow him to respond.

The doors were barely halfway open and I'd vacated the lift. Excruciating; and why did I say "all the best"? I never say 'all the best' to anyone, ever. I seem to come out with these obscure phrases I'd never use elsewhere. I have an uncontrollable issue with my speech. As long as my friends don't hear it, I suppose I can get away with it. Nobody pays attention to what I say anyway, unless it's a word I over-emphasise in my accent. Anything I say is hot air, which I don't mind at all.

We'll pick up from here shortly.

What's so funny?

It's no secret that London is one of the world's most multicultural cities. People exchange in dialects spanning from all countries, cities and towns, meaning there are infinite twists to the pronunciation of the English language. Yet it is when I open my mouth, people are taken aback. It's my accent that people claim to have difficulty understanding. Luckily I see it as more of an asset (yes I work in finance) than a hindrance. People will always remember the man (boy) with the chipper Scouse accent and enormous teeth (I'm still growing into them). I've encountered many who underestimate those with an accent that differs from received pronunciation, which only gives us the upper hand. They expect less, so we surprise more.

As my dad was a solicitor, growing up I saw the effect even the slightest accent had on posh men in suits. In his late-thirties, when I was between the age of eight and 11, he'd often receive calls from people with names like Sandy and Arthur late into the evening at home. We could be in the back garden, half an hour into our football session; I'd be setting up my hundredth free-kick to blast at the goal when the phone would ring from the garden table and ruin my moment. The ancient Nokia theme tune would turn my dad's (reasonably well-spoken) Liverpudlian accent into a classmate of Mark Fitzwilliam Darcy.

"This is Nick speaking."

The instant transformation would never fail to amuse me. I'd listen to the first sentence and dart inside shouting for my brother and sister.

"Phone voice! Phone voice!"

They would come running from opposite ends of the house screaming, "Nick speaking," over-pronouncing every syllable.

He'd do his best to shoo us away pretending to be angry, but it would never work. As we grew older, we'd learn when there was a time and place to take the piss out of 'this is Nick speaking' (obviously every time was the perfect time) – often we'd do it before he'd hung up. How could a mere phone call turn my joker of a dad, the biggest child in the world (who at the age of 54 climbed aboard a luggage rack on a train to claim he was a suitcase and therefore was not required to purchase a ticket from the conductor), into a completely different human; his professional self. Through these conversations, I was exposed to the greatest lie of all. This is the work laugh.

I struggled to comprehend what made my dad snigger in work discussions; even on the occasions when I heard full conversations, I couldn't get the humour. It just, well, wasn't funny. I've always sought to see the funny side of life because life without laughter wouldn't be fun (which is why we love to talk about people who take themselves too seriously behind their backs). I thought I couldn't possibly ever need to fake a laugh. I can laugh at anything because I'm still a child. However, there seems to be poison in the water of every office I've been in. It sucks any hope of having a laugh or the desire for enjoyment from all there. People turn up to get through the day. What's the point?

Surely I could laugh with these people.

I headed for the capital aged 20. I was unemployed, underachieving and aimless. I had no clue what I wanted to do, but I was haunted by the prospect of failure and still am. With a total of three months' work experience to my name and a Lower Second-Class Honours in accounting and financial management, I knew I'd have to be realistic, at least for the time being. We all do, don't we? I was never going to end up at a big bank. I couldn't code, so the tech titans were out of my reach. Marketing? They, like many, wouldn't look at me with my grade. I thought I had nowhere to turn until I was given a chance in a sales role. It was not only sales but working with people too; recruiting them to be precise. I talked my way through the interview – about how I craved interaction with others and how I felt my sporting background showed I had the ability to work in a team. All the usual nonsense we recite as we beg someone to pay us a little over £20,000 a year on the condition we earn them five times that. The notion of recruitment seemed easy; the double salary commission drew me in. I just had to reach my ludicrous target earnings.

I thought I'd entered into a light-hearted environment; the office had an enormous gong we could smack with each deal we made, this seemed fun? I approached my first ever full-time job optimistically. I was now an executive head hunter in the City.

My interview consisted of questions about football trivia and within an hour the formal offer came. I got to bang the gong while 'In The Air Tonight' by Phil Collins played. It felt so satisfying (of course I timed it perfectly with the drums). The entire office went for drinks to celebrate, it was three o'clock on a Friday, *"this is work?"* I thought. I couldn't wait to get started on Monday. It only took one week of interviewing and I'd landed a job; had I landed on my feet again? It all seemed so easy, I could see the success panning out in front of me – this was it. I already knew my life was going to be a stroll.

No chance.

I quickly realised, in fact, it would not be a stroll. I was forced to spend two blocks of two and a half hours uninterrupted making phone calls.

"PST! PST! PST!" The boss, whom I'm referring to, as Mr Windsor, would scream this twice a day.

Prime sales time – a time where I and the other two graduates weren't even allowed to go to the toilet unless something was coming out. This started from the afternoon of my first day. I'd call up a switchboard of a large financial firm and ask to be put through to a software developer, whose name I'd found online. I'd be put through to, usually, a socially awkward person going about their life as normal. About half would answer in a shy manner, to which I'd immediately begin to race through a script I'd rehearsed, offering them exciting roles with fantastic progression opportunities! Amazing. I had no idea whether they could progress or not, I just wanted commission. Phone call after phone call, rejection after rejection. It was utterly humiliating. Not even three weeks in and I'd realised the lie I'd been sold that Friday; the gong was banged a maximum of once a week by a much more experienced member of the firm. For five hours a day we'd recite our lines that were taught to us by Mr Windsor, "Good morning, my name is Andrew and I'm an executive hunter with the firm Pegasus," a successful conversation would last more than 30 seconds, a bad one would end with me being asked politely to "Just fuck off and delete my number, mate." I had one Oxford University computer science graduate ask me if I'd been to university and lecture me on how he was a "premium commodity". Sure thing chicken wing.

I am ignorant thus ignorance towards me angers me.

I was sick of the job within six weeks (it was more like two, but I don't want to sound like a baby. I'm not a baby, honestly I'm not). I'd do anything to make the days pass quicker including typing phone numbers into my desk phone as slowly as possible, in the hope it would accumulate across the day and waste a significant amount of time, which probably added up to about four minutes. This was not due to idleness; this was sadness. Disliking the idea of a job when you wake up is an experience most of us have, but disliking the actual job throughout the day and being so pathetic, you can't see it through because all you want is an easy life, is something far rarer. I was, and truly am this pathetic. If I had it my way I'd never work a day again, I repeatedly told myself every night; but I couldn't let the negativity towards the job show. I lived alone, in a flat I didn't pay for, with nothing to care about, but I was so spoilt and hard done by that I'd sit alone and feel sorry for myself, in one of the most entertaining cities in the world. I'm embarrassed by how sheltered I was (am). With the firm being just 12 strong, our City office space was humble, if I'm being polite. Three desks of two-by-two workstations had us facing our colleagues and in my case, the jumped-up Mr Windsor. A short man with a greying buzz cut. He'd made huge sums of money in the aftermath of the financial crisis, before the recruitment industry exploded onto the scene. With his success came enormous confidence in his professional self, he'd stand with his shoulders back and his head held as high as possible. He walked into the room with a swagger that was infectious to all but me. I just saw a man with glasses.

I could see through his falseness, high-fiving all those who worked under him upon entry, playing a song daily at five minutes to five before he left to return to his house in west London, despite us not being allowed to leave before six. In fact, if I left before six-thirty, he'd comment to me the next day, saying, "Well, I suppose you're contracted until six o'clock," as if I were to be ashamed of leaving so early.

But he would say such a comment with an enormous grin on his face, he'd chuckle after it, squinting his eyes and extending his neck forward. This was not light-hearted. It was false and felt like some sort of intimidation tactic. I wish I'd have reacted to this, out of my distaste for the job, out of my distaste for my own stupidity of falling for this lie, out of distaste for where I was at the time, but I learned irrational behaviour made me look weak. I learned that this is a game. I figured conversing through a forced smile threw Mr Windsor and the gang off my scent. I'd go about my work and when he approached, with one of his predictable jabs about me stealing his Rolex, or mimicking my accent, I'd laugh it off and return a safe comment to play along with Mr Windsor. I'd make him feel superior, as he desired, putting me in control. I learned to force out a cackle from my mouth, a sharp 'ts' sound followed by two or three 'ha has'. Subconsciously, I had given birth to my own work laugh; it stuck with me long after the nine-month employment tenure at Pegasus. It has grown, developed, and been perfected over the past few years as I've entered the financial sector, where the same, dull, predictable jokes about my city of origin are forced upon me. Again, I must laugh along with men in their late thirties as they joke about balance sheet items, company accounting methods, and the latest news in the *Financial Times*. Oh, and the only way I'd meet the Queen is through a charity project. Ts-ha-ha-ha.

What is it all for? I've found myself closing my eyes and questioning, *did I really just have a conversation about corporate governance for ten minutes*? I can't control my feelings towards my work, how can I? I have little interest in the minutia of a company's financial information. I don't care for company growth or financial projections for the forthcoming years, which is why I am so haunted by the feeling that I am playing my life safely, much too safely. I've taken minimal risks and pursued something I do not love, or even remotely enjoy. I haven't chased a dragon into its lair and put my life on the line, I've just played the role of the baker's boy learning a trade. I cannot fight the foul mood it brings, because there is no passion, no spark, no drive for what I am doing. *What am I even doing*? I ask myself. I spend hours scowling at a screen, frowning so intensely that three cracks have begun to engrave into my forehead. I'm meant to be youthful. At least I've got hair, albeit ginger. I waste my time, wishing I was following my dream of performing, be it in sport or on stage. I want to engage with people, I want to tell stories and create. I've done nothing to feed this desire; it's my own fault. Why do I purely wish and wonder? Why do I wait for nothing to happen, other than for a middle-aged halfwit (who has also waited for years on end and has given up) to encroach upon my space and engage in a conversation about the morning's business news story, regurgitating what he read during his commute on how company X has crashed into liquidation because the directors didn't understand pensions and intangible asset impairments properly. Of course I didn't read it. I have no interest, despite what my CV and covering letter said. Yet as I sit there helplessly, he unloads his 'expert insight' as to why the company went down the drain. He closes his monologue with a limp joke and awaits my response, which is a blank expression as I briefly evaluate my life for three-tenths of a second, followed by a forced ex-(ts)ha-ha-hale. My work laugh eats me up inside because it makes him think we are alike. We are not. I can't wait any longer for nothing. I must give up the act in work, but I'm not courageous enough.

Not one bit.

Work work work

I cannot help but dwell on the series of decisions that led me to an office job. Why do I continue to sell out? If I hate working in finance I should walk away. Do I live in fear that my parents will cut me off and stop contributing towards my rent if I quit? I could easily live in a smaller apartment, or a different location. But I'd rather be comfortable than at risk, which, in turn, makes me miserable. How can I moan for something more, when I'm too scared to tell my parents how sad I am? I'm a self-entitled shambles.

Following my conversation with Lee Gi (we're back), I began thinking of how I could change my life. *What could I really do to change all of this? I can't quit. I'm contracted and will have to pay my tuition and exam fees back, but I can make a start, surely. What can I do?* I was having a shower conversation with myself, but while walking in the office (with clothes on). *I can write, I can plot out a script for the hit show I planned (we all have one), I can start a business, or go to night school, I can utilise my spare time constructively. I'm only 24. I have more energy now than I'll ever have. I need to work for me, towards my own goals and stop letting my life pass me by.* It was something along those lines (though I'll be honest, there's a slight chance it's not word for word). I think it was a proverbial penny dropping. It'd come from a great height and through a thick bed of fog, but it collided with my brain on this particular morning. All thanks to Lee Gi. Though I had no idea, I realised, whatever I was going to do, I just had to have a go. I had a revelation.

My stride elongated with this newfound purpose. I was completely overcome. I was going to work tirelessly at this. I was going to obsess in chasing what I wanted. I felt like I was going to rule the w-

"Sorry, I'm so sorry."

Stopped dead in my tracks; cue more lying. I cannot turn a corner in work without interrupting another person's path. Every corner I turn, every door I open, there's an obstacle to deal with. It's a metaphor for my life. I can never pass someone without uttering the word 'sorry'. I can't control it. It's in my weedy DNA to offer an unnecessary apology for no reason at all. There are times when I walk past people in a corridor big enough for us to each walk our dog and I am incapable of passing them without uttering 'sorry'. Even if it's with a whisper or a whimper, I must apologise. I am not apologetic for passing someone, so why must I offer my apologies? I feel almost subservient when using it, pathetic for my over-the-top politeness, at least I know what it is. I know what I am. The word 'sorry' is another needless lie I've witnessed throughout my life, such as when people open with, 'I'm terribly sorry, but' – the fourth and final word is the indicator that the first three were untrue, they aren't sorry. I can't even make the 60-second walk from the lift to my desk without a couple of little 'sorry' lies on my part. Another reason to hate myself. At least I'm amused by own tragic state. I'm at ease with myself, or I would be if I stopped saying 'sorry'.

I don't know why I've pretended I have a desk. I do not. I'm part of a pathetic hot desk workstation situation. Before I begin the frantic scramble for a seat (cost-cutting – times are hard) I must stop the raging heat my body is still generating from the morning commute. Each strand of hair is moist and my scalp saturated. The only cooling sensation I have is where my damp clothes meet my skin, which is radiating scorching heat from my body. I can feel my skin is blotchy and red, the bags under my eyes feel like they are holding puddles of water. I can't remove my jacket first thing in the morning, as I'm suspicious of sweat patches no matter what colour shirt I'm sporting. Keep it on until ten o'clock is my policy or go to the toilet for a little spot check.

Not a soul in my team will say good morning to me, but I am accustomed to this. I've come to realise the advantages of being invisible in the morning. I can remain in my world, away from work, thinking of a way out as if I am a prisoner. I cannot show my true feelings. My professional self works on autopilot to allow effortlessly dealing with colleagues when necessary. I just wish he'd be as assertive as I think I am, instead, he's a weasel. Even though it's a hot desk set-up, I still have My Desk. It's mine. My headphones will remain in and no attempt at eye contact will be given until after ten o'clock. I'll envision a beach to take my mind away. The tender sound of shallow waves rippling; a Coke (plenty of ice, no lemon, never lemon) to sip on as I lay down under the sun, letting ocean water dry on my body. What I'd do to escape this painfully average life.

I daydream habitually in work, longing for my life to change without having to take charge myself and launch in a new direction. Why can't it be easy? In the world of mergers and acquisitions (boring finance jargon for companies buying or selling parts of other companies or whole companies; like when Facebook purchased WhatsApp for $19 bn), days are distinguished by the length of time spent in the office. During live deal engagements, leaving the office before eight o'clock is a good day, far from ideal, but, especially as a young employee, it is normal to be kept in well past eight. I've already highlighted the lack of control over how busy we are (or how busy we're kept). Our day is dictated to us by those higher up the archetypal food chain, though an office is nothing like the wild, there is zero survival instinct, just an enclosed pen of overfed bulls storming around marking their territory. Anyone beneath them is sucking up to make their own lives simpler in this horrid relationship. We must wait to be ordered around, told to jump and how high, then forced to jump twice, all with a smile on our face and being thankful for being allowed to be in the same room.

To make matters worse, I have rather sensitive nostrils, which is a curse when the person dictating my day decides to take off his shoes under the desk space that separates us. Unsurprisingly this winds me up two-fold. Firstly, because I have to bite my tongue, and secondly, I have to hold my breath and look to the ceiling to avoid the stench of the sweaty socks. At least the trainer wearers change their shoes and keep their feet covered throughout the day. Sitting with nothing but socks on in an enclosed public space (I'll allow planes) is ignorant beyond belief. Feet stink. Inexcusable. Nobody wants to see, smell or taste your sweaty socks.

Cheers.

I've always been intrigued by the idea of being a partner at a professional services firm. Granted they work incredibly hard and are trenemdous at their jobs. But isn't that true of anyone after 15 years plus of service in the same role? For some (emphasis on 'some' being a small minority) partners it feels like because they've done the same thing for long enough (boring), they have progressed onto the next stage by right. If you stay in one location for long enough and know the correct circle of people, it'll happen. But, what do I know? I just dislike senior people who have self-entitled boisterousness on the floor. Strolling around knowing they, partially, own the place. I've witnessed a man in his early forties shout across the floor, "You haven't got me a cookie?"

This was to his secretary. Like a spoilt six-year-old waiting for their mother to return from the shop. I've probably said it to my mum in the past (I prefer crisps to a cookie, not really got a sweet tooth). It's hypocritical to claim I dislike white men in suits, when I, on occasion am a white man in a suit, but there is a distinct difference in generational and geographical upbringing. This difference is no more apparent than on the last Thursday of every month – work drinks. Thirsty Thursday's; inventive, isn't it? It rolls off the tongue. Of course, if my mates in Liverpool knew I walked around asking people, "Thirsty Thursday?", they'd send me into the Thames headfirst; I'm not even worth dumping in the River Mersey.

There's a unique feel to the office on a Thirsty Thursday (more a unique smell). I can sense the extra two or three sprays of aftershave and perfume. Some potent scents are flaunted. I'll be able to notice who's lapped on an extra helping of their favourite sprays before work, why is that? Out on the prowl are we? Even the people with kids are at it. The concoction of several eau de toilettes and eau de parfums singe my nostrils, I'll be squinting and sneezing for the whole day. Seven hours with my nose like a leaking tap. Roll on four o'clock. Early finishes are the longest days. I'll check my watch every three minutes from about ten o'clock. The minute hand appears to be going backwards as I count the passing seconds. Ten-minute breaks turn into 30-minute sessions away from my desk. I become increasingly restless as the day wears on. All is well, however because I know the time will come.

I comfort myself with the thought that time doesn't exist[2] unless you're a physicist (I am not). I'm referring to our measurement of time. The watch I stare at is a product of our own imagination (and somebody else's genius). I could leave earlier than four o'clock. I'll leave when my own time is right. How can something non-existent control our lives? How can we submit ourselves and give our own lives to fiction? We must arrive at work at a common time suited to other people. We must slave hard to make their money at the expense of our time. We must abide by common laws established by others or face punishment. If I were alive several thousand years ago, I wouldn't know these pressures. I'd learn to fight, hunt, or a trade (probably a trade let's be honest). Yet I've been born into this world and live at this age and am apparently so privileged to be doing so. All I do is sit around and hate the position I'm in. Perhaps I am wasting the life I am so incredibly fortunate to have, working towards something I do not believe in. Why can't I offer more than such measly thoughts of self-pity and sorrow?

Forget all that. I'm parched.

---

2. Time exists.

Chapter III – Drink up, drink up

Thursday is the new Friday

Friday night is for our real friends. Thursday night is Friday night with our colleagues. Knowing there's just one more alarm call until the weekend fills the body with a warm feeling. We can forget our responsibilities and relish ignoring work emails, messages, clients, colleagues we cannot bear and anything else dictating our lives throughout the working week. In the eager anticipation of the weekend, which so many of us live for, we can accept going for drinks with said colleagues. Anything to escape the walls of the workplace we're confined to. It's quite the networking event, getting to know people outside of the office; their true selves. Friends of colleagues will even be accepted to prepare for the big push over the final hurdle. Networking is the business buzzword of the modern era. We're relentlessly reminded that the most important thing to do is expand our networks. It essentially involves offering one's CV to another in a short conversation, blowing as much smoke up our own backside as possible on the off-chance that, in the future, however distant, we cross paths and can use the familiarity to promote our self-interests. "Remember when we met?" It's another façade involving nothing more than puffing our own chests out and attempting to leave a lasting impression on someone's mind in as little time as possible. Being someone who isn't the greatest fan of small talk (not that any of us are), I can't say I avidly attempt to network. Networking is not merely speaking to somebody new. Unfortunately, it involves talking about work, as if we were a shop window advertising to a passer-by, hence my complete distaste for it. I'm not keen to advertise something I hate myself for, much like a celebrity not advertising a potential drug addiction (not until they need to spark a comeback anyway).

Nevertheless, at work drinks we must go through the motions of meeting friends of colleagues and reluctantly talk about work and experiences of the past; as long as we're away from the office, I suppose. Being disinterested makes me seem almost awkward, but I'm disinterested because I have the same conversation with each new person. It's mind-numbing. They'll usually open by asking where I'm from; as I say, Liverpool, they'll acknowledge that they would have guessed, as unbelievably they could tell from my accent. After years of the same question and reaction, I have to consciously prevent myself from rolling my eyes all the way back to Liverpool. Next I'm hit with the dreaded, "So you're a Liverpool fan?" Oh dear.

When a child is born in Liverpool, before their interests are established, before they learn to walk or talk, potentially even have a name, it is decided we are either a red or a blue. Liverpool or Everton. It transcends anything in the city: politics, race, religion. Nothing compares to the rivalry of Everton and Liverpool. The most bitter of Everton fans raised me, something I'm both grateful and miserable for. Everton is the lesser successful team in the city; they have a much smaller fan base and they are the smaller club (it hurt to write that). There is a sense of nobility about those who support Everton, in the sense that we take hardship in supporting a less successful club that belongs to the people of our city. The classic British support for the underdog. In my lifetime, Everton have managed to win one trophy, when I was nine months old. Other than that, there have just been a few comings close.

Supporting Everton Football Club has been more of a travesty than a tragedy. As they say, it's the hope that kills you. It's like being on a night out and getting invited to the after party of a girl (or boy) you half-fancy on your course in the first year of university (when you've not kissed anyone) and getting really excited about where the night could up. Only to realise it was a genuine party invite and you're introduced to the person they're sleeping with as a course mate. The party is also awful and you know nobody else there, so you find yourself trying to get away as quickly as possible to cut all ties from the block of flats and save what's left of your wounded pride. But as you make an escape to your own block, you spot somebody, unconscious, face down next to the central pond of the halls of residence and covered in their own sick. *I can't ignore her and leave her face down,* you tell yourself, even though you just want to go to bed. You can't pretend to not see somebody face down covered in their own sick. You try to aid the girl who continues to vomit so you call 1-1-1 (not 9-9-9 as you're not a maniac) and summon the good paramedics to collect her. They eventually whisk her away so you can go home to clean her sick off your shoes and mend your broken heart. Supporting Everton, you find yourself going out with all the hope in the world, only to find yourself going through a fresh pair of shoes each week as they're covered in someone else's barf. Pathetic isn't it?

For someone to assume I'm a Liverpool fan breaks my heart. It would be easy for me to support the bigger, more successful club. My life would be free of the torment. But through sorrow, we are given hope and it's the hope of what might happen that we live for. The assumption of me supporting Liverpool also winds me up because ultimately, too many people who have no affiliation to the city pretend support them because "Dad went to uni there." Do me a favour. Thus in the capital, I tend to skip through the questions about my accent and my football allegiance as quickly as possible.

Drink please.

The prestige

Prestige is so important to many who take themselves too seriously and drinks events are the perfect time to show off. The worst time of the year to go for drinks is in winter, without a doubt. Not because of the freezing cold, or because the only daylight I get to experience is my walk to Angel tube station in the morning – no. It's because winter is ski season and southerners love skiing. Really love it. Skiing is so much fun: stunning views, crisp air in your lungs as you fly down a mountain with your friends, accompanied by tonnes of booze, and more importantly, incredible food (I don't shag cheese but I quite like a raclette).

To the more pretentious Londoners, it's so much more. Whispers around the office of California, double black diamonds in Canada, several resorts in Les Alps (that's French for the Alps), it's all they talk about from November onwards; joy. All I want after a long day with my first sip of lager is a mundane chat about life, something to take the edge off. Skiing patter turns into a flat-out competition between men (it's always men) finding out who has the most impressive ski resort portfolio. One particular work event is fixed into my memory; one of the cross-team networking events. This is where those who work in the same function but are aligned to different sectors (i.e. doing the same dance to different music in the disco) meet for drinks as they can establish common ground through doing the same day job, but have different clients. (I analyse and write reports on media and tech companies, whereas another sector group would be food and beverage companies or insurance companies or investment banks for example.) What is it, same-same but different? Anyway, it's wholly awkward but drinks are paid for and so was our social activity. They always lure us in with something like mini-golf, bowling, virtual reality gaming or dart throwing. (Usually fantastic entertainment for all the family to be fair.) I was enjoying my first exhale after the first sip of beer (thinking about trying to not get too drunk and embarrassing myself somehow), enjoying the elongated 'Ah' sound as I toasted myself for nearly making it through another dreadful week; all means to an end. My colleague, a guy called Toby and his posh friend approached me. Thinking I could trust Toby, I was happy to engage politely in a conversation that no doubt I wouldn't want to be a part of.

His friend (who's part of one of the same-same but different teams, the team that despite doing the same job as us think they're investment bankers on Wall Street in the eighties, cool fellas) swaggered up to me. I shook his hand and force a grin, mouth filled following another swift swig of my beer. I offered a raise of the eyebrow to greet him.

"Good to meet you, I'm Monty." Monty, short for Montague.

Of course his name is Montague. I knew enough about him before we'd even begun (we'll get to judgement and misjudgement much later). His non-lace loafers and Oxford shirt with sleeves rolled up all the way and his slicked-back hair suggested he was the type who loves putting on a good old-fashioned 'Ralphie'; definitely wears boat shoes all year round and pretends to like whisky. He seemed like the kind of person who desires to be in a members' club. At least half of London professionals, aged 21 to 30, dress up in exactly the same attire unless they're out to dinner with their parents, in which they will wear a blazer and tie. I'll come to judgement at a later point, but it's easy to spot a Monty (Montague) from a mile away. Nonetheless, I'm not rude, so I was happy to smile and fake my way through a conversation.

He asked, "Which part of the firm do you work in then?"

Another go-to question (despite us being at an event specifically for our teams), but at least he accepted the accent for what it is, so I continued. I thought perhaps Montague defies the status quo of the 50%. We exchanged our CVs verbally for a minute with Toby weighing in, linking the conversation mutually. It all seemed relatively bearable (but dull), until, "You been out on the slopes much recently, Monty?" Monty being short for Montague, in case I forgot to mention.

Why did he have to ask?

My interest in the conversation took a dive. As someone who has been skiing only a handful (well, less than two handfuls and mostly to Les Alps, which again is French for the Alps) of times, I adore it, but I do not feel a rush of blood between my legs when discussing it, unlike Monty (Montague) here. The twinkle in his eye gave away his hand, He was an absolute powderhound, no doubt and he was getting ready to tell us all about it. I was helpless.

"Managed to get out to Val d'Isère (it's always Val d'Isère) a couple of times since Christmas, the snow has been unbelievable this year, probably going to head again in a couple of weeks because this season has just been pure powder."

Here lies my issue. Skiing is fantastic, it is endless fun from being on the slopes to the 'apres-ski', but why must I be lectured on the quality of the snow? This is how to tell if someone is truly pretentious. They won't stop offering their assessment on the quality of the snow from their skiing holidays. Now, I'm unsure what these people expect when they book a skiing holiday 3,000 metres and beyond above sea level, in winter, but I think we would all expect there to be snow present. It's almost an elitist comment to make, made by those who want to show their knowledge of skiing because it's their 'thing'. But wow, they make it dull. The snow is always unbelievable as well; it's never poor in quality (unless you were in Morzine in March 2019, it wasn't up to much because it rained the day after a massive snowfall, also known as a 'dump' to Monty, short for Montague). Sometimes, I think it may just be because it is snow that falls weekly. Don't get me started on if you meet someone who has been skiing in Japan and tells you that because the air is warmer the snow is pure powder over there, pure powder (I've been told this by at least four people, Toby included but we still like Toby). Okay, we get it, you like snow. What can be said in response to someone who is supposedly so fixated on the standard of snow they ski on, up a mountain, where there is unlimited snow. Again, what do they expect? I've never known anyone come back from a walking trip and comment on the firmness of the footpath. Do people sample the snow while they're up there? Do they take a test tube with them for a sample and masturbate while cradling it later, climaxing as they pour the powdery solution over themselves? It becomes more ridiculous when, somehow, if other skiers are present, they feel the need to compete about the quality of the snow they experienced; and often, they're talking about in the neighbouring resort. It makes me want to scream. But I'd somehow be the outcast of the conversation for simply not caring about the quality of snow. It's snow.

Having said that, I love it when it's pure powder after a massive overnight dump.

All I could offer in response was a smile so forced that my cheeks quivered as I watched Monty (Montague) and Toby list the plethora of destinations they'd been skiing. Being stuck in a conversation with keen skiers is quite the honey trap. Sounds fun, but you get stuck quickly. I've never spoken about my summer holiday to South-East Asia or felt the need to list every country my passport has been stamped in over the last five years (even if it is over 20. I won't brag, but, Vietnam, Thailand, Mexico, Bali, UAE, India, United States many times, obviously all over Europe as well, but I don't need to compete; South Africa as well). I find it excruciating being a passenger in a conversation with others, just observing two people chat, as opposed to me being in a conversation and getting the attention I deserve. All I could do was stare into my glass after each sip, waiting for it to sink low enough for me to excuse myself. Situations as such are potentially why I always end up slurring my words within two hours of going for work drinks. My mind wants to numb itself from the surrounding falseness and competition for which I have no interest because I'm not one of them, am I?

(South Africa was a safari holiday by the way; it was so spiritual, you know?)

After five excruciating minutes, I took the double gulp to finish my pint.

"Refill anyone?"

I hate that I am too polite to not offer, if only I was rude enough to sort myself, I'd avoid so much of this. I thought the worst had passed with Monty (Montague). We were surely set to move on to better things, as long as politics wasn't to be brought up (politics isn't a good mixer for alcohol). At the bar, I had a moment of clarity to calm myself, no thought of top ski spots and mid-mountain bars to drink at, or which places serve amazing fondue. I could sort myself another drink and have a moment in my own head, planning the conversation upon my return with my pint of lager and their two pints of London crafted ale (obviously).

As I waited, I took a moment to scan across the area reserved for our firm; looking for conversations I could join and not want to glass my face after four minutes. It's surprising when out of the office just how many people I want to avoid, mainly due to the fear of small talk, or worse, work talk. I returned to the dynamic duo, clutching my normal pint glass of lager between their jam jars of hipster juice and I was welcomed to a conversation that had moved on from skiing. Bliss. Toby turned to me.

"Monty was just talking about the people in our team."

I had no other response, other than, "Right, okay," and I nodded towards Monty (short for Montague) as if to hand him an imaginary microphone.

"There's some talent in your team, like that one over there."

It had gotten worse than skiing.

Commenting on colleagues makes my skin crawl, not because I'm morally just, but because the only reason we're in social situations is that we work together, otherwise we wouldn't want to know each other. The thought of it makes me feel weird. I didn't know Monty well so couldn't help but feel uncomfortable. He was closer to 35 than 20 and was commenting on women who had barely started a graduate programme. "Talent." I sipped deep into the glass as I thought of a response to the situation. Monty (Montague) was sniggering away. I should have commented on his gut and non-prescription lenses (obviously) ruining any chance he had, but I'm too polite. He hadn't said anything to her or offended her, so there was no need to comment. I was drawing a blank, so pointed towards Toby.

"You've fancied her since you walked in," buying myself time. (That right there, is banter.)

Expertly, I'd shifted the focus towards someone else without looking like I wanted to be Mr 21st century. Plus it's fun to put people on their back foot, watching them 'umm, ah' and squirm as they worm their way out from being put on the spot.

Something as trivial as a joke about being attracted

to somebody comes with a short essay and a PowerPoint presentation about why that is factually incorrect. Though if it were true they'd be able to woo the subject in question. Why can't people laugh at themselves? I'm so pathetic I get nervous about answering a phone call from an unknown number, but at least I can acknowledge it. These people cannot relax. The conversation dried up, unfortunately, far quicker than my ability to drink a pint of lager. Finding excuses to duck out of a conversation is difficult for me; I've such a big mouth so it's obvious when I've nothing to say. I allowed the two to drool over the graduate while I stared at nothing, offering an empty smile anytime I heard a chuckle. How to get out of this?

It's handy having a colleague who makes the days go quicker, the one who calls for a break just as you're thinking about one; the Gareth to our David Brent (I needed to get one reference from *The Office* in). Office jobs are only bearable if you've got good people around you. We all need somebody in there to keep us stay sane. In my blank stare away from the chuckle brothers, My Gareth caught my eye. He'd entered without me knowing. I thought he was staying late at work. The weight pulling my neck down to the ground fell away.

"I'm just going to catch up over there."

Without awaiting a response, or wishing him or his craft ale well, I walked away from Monty (Montague). He'd had his moment and blown it all over a graduate. I strode over to My Gareth; finally, someone I can be myself with.

Gareth

We all have one[3]. Our Gareth is the one with whom we can be honest, with whom we can delve into the weird and really

---

3. I actually worked here with my best mate of ten years and we shared a Gareth between us, but that doesn't make for a good story.

weird, firing off on multiple tangents because we know no matter how much garbage we spout, it's just a colleague relationship. We'd never go out with them over the weekend (again, they're for real friends), but we're more than happy to have a few drinks after work. It's great when we meet someone in work who feels the same as us. They have some sort of common interest and seem relatively human, thus we can relax in their presence, instead of using our professional selves. It's a match made in heaven. Drinks after work become a laugh with someone, not quite a friend, but a good colleague. We think we know them well because they tell us whom they've slept with recently, or use their girl/boyfriend's name openly with us (I pretend to know everything about the individual despite always feeling slightly strange each time their name is brought up). I know the shows his girlfriend watches and that she doesn't like him going out without her. I even know their bi-monthly copulating schedule as he comes in twinkly-eyed and brings up, "Had sex when we got back on Saturday," like having sex with a long-term partner is an achievement (we all know it is really).

All the while I have no idea what she looks like or who she really is; could be imaginary. I'd never know. But a relationship at work puts us at ease, opening a sliver of our lives to someone, allowing us to be slightly vulnerable and feel human. I've even debated asking My Gareth if he wants to go out on a Friday, then realising the conversation would be over by half ten and we'd have to go home, therefore held back. Terrible idea.

When My Gareth caught my eye at the bar, I knew I had an escape route from Monty (Montague)'s Guide to Picking Up Chicks. I skipped over to My Gareth who was instantly into conversation with one of the more approachable of the work lot; plain sailing from here. My Gareth was with the person in the office who would always come for a drink, but never suggest one, an ever-present but not a leader, a bit of an unsung hero around the workplace.

I joined a conversation about medical treatments. No clue how they'd got there but it was happening. Given the previous 15 minutes, I was more than happy to go along with it. I believe when approaching a conversation I have to wait long enough before I can wade in with a comment. After I've been welcomed, I must listen for half a minute or so, earn my stripes by nodding my head intently while pushing for eye contact to allow myself in when we're all comfortable. It's quite the unspoken formality. Why two grown men were discussing Caesareans is beyond me, maybe it was the beer (no craft ale in sight now, these are good people). With my girlfriend being a doctor and having been involved directly with the procedure dozens of times, I am (un)officially qualified to talk about the subject no matter my level of personal experience in the field. Illness and medicine are a funny topic of conversation for non-medically qualified professionals. If we've experienced something personally, we're experts on the matter. For example, I know that a strong medicine for Crohn's disease is 150 mg of Azathioprine daily and that the medicine has an effect on your skin in sunlight, therefore those taking it need to wear a high factor and expect to get hives when they so much as blink at the sun. We like to offer our deepest knowledge and share it with others. Why this is I'll never know; it's in our competitive nature.

So, because my girlfriend is a doctor (just need to keep hammering that one home and hope she doesn't leave me), I feel like I have the equivalent of, if I'm being modest, roughly three years of medical training. After a few nods and some elongated eye contact to show I'd been silently accepted, I finally weighed in with my expert knowledge.

"Do you know they tear the skin so it heals quicker?"

I felt so powerful as they each turned towards me. I could

see they were in awe of what I had to say. Here I am, a mere 24-year-old miracle worker. How many strings I must have to my proverbial bow I could see them thinking, 'Is there anything he can't do? His teeth are perfect as well.' Then came the much-anticipated response. My Gareth nearly spat his drink in my face laughing, to which I was completely bemused. I couldn't understand, so sipped hard on my beer and stared deeply into the floor (this happens too often), to allow him a chance of explaining himself.

"No they don't at all, my wife has had one and her skin wasn't torn, that's total bollocks!"

I was taken aback because My Gareth had turned on me so quickly, the absolute traitor. But here lies the difference between a friend and a colleague. With friends, there is no competition because we're all pathetic. We can laugh at each other and it's no harm, but when a colleague (incorrectly) calls me out in front of someone, to belittle me, I take offence. I was now on the back foot.

There's another fundamental issue with professional people as in this tale – they mistake their intelligence and ability to be good at their job, with being all-knowledgeable across all disciplines and are dismissive to those who say things they don't agree with or understand. I've had shoulder surgery, this doesn't mean I know how to cut cartilage away from a rotator cuff. I can regurgitate the sentence because it's engrained in my mind, but what that means or how it's done, I have no idea, as I only have three years of medical training and not a medical degree with foundation years and further surgical training. But what could I say in response? I had no proof.

"My girlfriend has performed a fair few as she's a doctor and she reliably informs me…"

My Gareth interrupted, "That's total bullshit, they don't tear a woman's skin open."

So, My Gareth (zero years of medical training) called a woman with nine years of medical training out on bullshit for how a Caesarean is performed. Why was I even having this discussion? I bet the ski goers were having a right laugh talking about how much they could leg press, or how many girls they've chopped; anything, at least they were having fun. I'd only had a couple of lagers and (being such a lightweight after two or three pints it really is a struggle to act rationally) somehow, I'd allowed a person with absolutely no medical knowledge (as opposed to my three years of training) to convince me that a doctor had lied to me about the performance of a Caesarean. Not only a doctor but the woman I live with (she's so medically qualified). Is this the only thing she's lied to me about? I took out my phone and began texting her. Idiot.

Me: "Why did you lie to me about women's vaginas being ripped for a Caesarean?"

Dr Girlfriend: "What are you on about?"

She had a point.

Me: "You said they tear the skin. Someone in work told me his wife had one and they cut it and now I'm being laughed at."

Dr Girlfriend: "They make a small initial incision and tear the skin from there because it heals better. I've been involved with probably over a hundred, unless he can do it better than I can. Though I'm guessing he didn't watch, nor has he done one."

Accompanying the message was a YouTube video of a Caesarean being performed, I wouldn't recommend you go searching for it. YouTube really has a video for everything.

She had a point.

I was hit by the fear. The feeling of, '*oh no, what have I done here?*' Knowing I'd made a complete fool of myself to someone I cared about over something so trivial. I decided I couldn't trust colleagues. I hated myself, I hated my job and I needed to walk away. But I had to get my point across. I couldn't let this go. I shoved my phone in My Gareth's direction.

"See, she's just said and she has performed them."

I was raging inside. I could feel the heat in my face from the embarrassment of all this because someone I had trust in had called me out on bullshit. The ever-present didn't even care. He had just come for a drink after work to get away from the office and had to bear witness to two people argue over something neither had the slightest clue about (other than my private medical training).

My Gareth shut it down with a, "We'll agree to disagree."

The cheek of it. What I said was a scientific fact; he couldn't disagree with it. I had to let go and allow the situation to die down and mull it over in my own time. I've never forgotten it, clearly. Embarrassing me like that in front of a colleague who definitely didn't care. He was too polite to take sides; he just wanted a drink after work. I thought of a genius comment about me having shoulder surgery but only being able to perform it about 30 seconds too late while arguing in my own head. The best comebacks pop into my head when it's too late, sometimes it's 30 seconds, sometimes it's a couple of days while in the shower. My rule of thumb is anything under a minute you can throw in, not that I care anyway. Still, I threw it into the conversation as I was drunk enough that talking rubbish was allowable. Bringing up my own medical experiences means I can talk about myself a bit more, which is one of my favourite hobbies. When talking about my surgery, I take care to play up to my proneness to injury and my countless pathetic injuries, as opposed to the medical hypochondriacs who tell us the stories of the time they were climbing Everest and survived an avalanche because their jacket got caught on a branch, when in reality they slipped on the path trekking in Delamere Forest looking for squirrels.

While telling my rather uneventful story about dislocating my shoulder playing football, I could see My Gareth itching to get a word in. My story is no valiant war tale to tell, just an injury-prone lanky mess falling over his own feet. I eased up to let him speak; what did he want to say?

"I had an operation a few years ago, had to get a dick transplant to make mine bigger."

No words.

Thirty-three years of age he was. I was stunned. The ever-present didn't know where to look and neither of us could even fake a work laugh, which made things worse. I turned to my pint yet again, as I knew a work laugh wouldn't get me out of this one. I couldn't believe how I had such enormous trust in someone. I thought I knew him. I thought he was like me, but not at all. A dick transplant, seriously? Of all the jokes he could have made. This is why colleagues can't be friends. This is why I don't invite them out with me, because of dick transplants. It was far too late to laugh. The conversation was drier than my mouth with morning breath. My Gareth knew he'd disgraced himself and he invited a couple more colleagues to steer us into a new direction as quickly as possible. I'd had enough and started thinking about home time, I had a quick and extremely obvious check of my watch (didn't care what time it was), pretended I'd lost track of time, and finished my drink. I had no plans but knew I should leave after the joke ruined my night and possibly my week. But the alcohol was taking its toll, it wanted me to stay out. It only ever takes two or three pints to consume and control me. I knew I'd regret it Friday morning when I'd be back behind my trio of screens saturated by my own sweat, but the feeling of alcohol is too powerful and too seductive. I knew I could stay for another. One for the road?

After giving in to the need for one more, I shifted my focus back towards the conversation, which had charged on without me while I debated in my head. They were now frothing over another corporate obsession, Amex points. We were in the pits of conversation. People carry American Express credit cards like it gives them status, even though the vast majority receive them free of charge in work. It's rare to go out in London without one big timer asking if the particular establishment they're in accepts Amex. The rule is you take your Amex out to show everybody you have an Amex and then you ask, 'Do you take Amex?' It's a credit card; I don't understand the obsession. Yes, I've got a black one obviously, but I never ask, I just pay quietly using my Apple Pay and if it gets rejected well then aren't I a massive dickhead. People talk about them like it's a members' club, like the card represents some form of exclusivity, 'I got 4,000 points when I booked my flights to Washington in January,' how fascinating, why would anybody want to be a part of that conversation? I suppose it's the genius of marketing and behavioural economics, like the fly on men's urinals to improve people's aim thus reducing cleaning costs of male lavatories. Don't be impressed by me knowing this, it's the first thing that came up when I searched 'behavioural economics' for an essay in university.

Right on cue, I was handed another pint free of charge. Free drinks will never get old. *Last one this time*, I told myself. I'm unsure why I go so weird when I realise I'm tipsy. I can feel my own mind begin to converse with itself in an attempt to reassure me that I'm okay. Whoever said 'less is more' has clearly never had a decent drink. I was happy to be a passenger of the Amex conversation because I would rather wax my undercarriage and eat the strips than join in, but I couldn't drink alone at an event. I had to stick around and sip away. When I hit a threshold of drunkenness I begin to play games in my own head, games that amuse me and clearly no one else. When I find myself surrounded by colleagues, I pick up on the business jargon that's thrown around and text them to my best friend (the one who I was lucky enough to have worked with for a couple of years).

Corporate jargon is a set of phrases people pick up and subconsciously spread throughout their network. Phrases like 'Let's touch base' – okay Officer. Where does it come from? 'We don't need to reinvent the wheel' is the white-hot phrase, even those who don't speak English as a first language use it, closely followed by not needing to 'boil the ocean'. It just reminds me of the lack of imagination and identity in this world. People would rather conform to using the language of an outdated world. I wonder when the first person commented on a particular piece of information 'moving the needle' or not on the greater aspect of a financial deal. Did they know they'd coined such a well-known phrase? I'd be trademarking it. Why would someone not bring his or her own dialect to a conversation? Our own language is what makes us unique, but being unique in this sector makes others uncomfortable and that's all people in this world ever want – their own comfort. Obviously, when I bring my own language, people accuse me of stealing something or coming from poverty and it's really funny.

The dullness of Amex points hit me hard and I knew that home was calling. It wasn't meant to be a good night. I thought of home. I had someone there waiting for me to give me attention and affection (so I believe after a drink). Someone I like, who doesn't talk like predictive text, someone who doesn't care about Amex points (because I get them all), or the quality of the Alpine snow; she just likes skiing because it's fun. Someone who laughs at my jokes and enjoys my accent without feeling the need to analyse it. This is where I want to be. Pitiful, isn't it? Evenings out with work rarely last over a few hours because conversations dry up when we realise that we have nothing in common but the desire to be wealthy. But because people don't talk openly about their desires, it's easy to drift away for someone, or something more appealing; like my own flat.

Chapter IV – Let's go home

Home-home

Where is home? I suppose currently it's the flat in Angel, London. The one with the birdbath and a bedroom so small I can almost touch every wall at the same time. I'm being dramatic; my limbs would each have to be two or three feet longer, it's small though. I love it really, but it feels temporary, yet another stopgap. It's my third flat in three years and I've no hope of buying given the average house price in my area is well over £1 million. Home-home is Liverpool. I'm so lucky to be from a city as incredible as Liverpool; somewhere so welcoming. I adore my home and burst with pride to have grown up there. Though rather annoyingly, my soft accent makes some people think I'm from a place outside of the city called Wirral, which is a bit like saying to Victoria Beckham, 'Didn't you used to be in Atomic Kitten?'

It's difficult to use the word 'home' when referring to London given the insincerity of it all. It feels like I'm betraying Liverpool, though that stems from my mum crying when I told her I was getting the train home when back in Liverpool – I mean home – visiting her. Yes, London is amazing, but friends are a 40-minute tube ride away; I can't just pop round for a cup of tea (not that I drink tea) and a natter about who shagged who or what's good on Netflix. I've got to accept talking about it in a group chat (or if I'm lucky a conference call) while sat in my flat craving human interaction and attention. Meeting friends has to be a thoroughly planned event and there's always someone who's busy. There's more chance of us all meeting for dinner on Mars than in Soho on a Thursday in the forthcoming two months.

We define home in different ways. Most class it as where they live, others, refer to the place they were born and spent their childhood. I wouldn't want to live in one city for my entire life, hence my desire to move to the capital. When someone leaves the city they grew up in, certain lifetime locals seem to take offence to it, as if those who've left have turned their back on home. I've been hit with a 'not surprised you've moved to London' before in a bar, as if I thought upping sticks for ten or so years made me better than the people that chose to stay (though technically me turning the other cheek and laughing it off makes me the better person here). I just assumed home would always be there, so why not explore a different city? Every city is the same. Some are content with staying locally their whole life, defending the honour of the city at all costs and they can't seem to understand why somebody would relocate. And some choose to explore and leave, sometimes with the hope of returning, but sometimes it lasts a lifetime. It's no harm to anyone, other than the lifetime locals who spend their life telling everybody the city they're from is the best despite never changing postcodes in their entire life.[4]

My home will always be Liverpool. Above all, home is where the dog is. Part of my love for returning home is knowing my dog is waiting to see me, knowing his little tail will wag uncontrollably as my parents point at me saying 'it's the Andrew' (the dog wouldn't know it was me if they just said 'it's Andrew'. I think it's because English is his second

---

4. My dad moved into the fifth house he'd ever lived in at the age of 37. It was the first time the first three characters of his postcode had changed and he'd moved less than a quarter of a mile from his fourth house. He's not a fist-waving 'Scouse not English' warrior, he just likes the area and between us, he's a bit of a mummy's boy so kept close to the house he grew up in. Pathetic. He still pays most of my rent.

language that there's a need for me being referred to as 'the Andrew'). He runs towards me sniffing and sneezing all over me as I bend down on all fours for a cuddle. This will always be home. Charwelton Last Fling, known dearly to us as Bobby; who is, without a doubt, the best-looking dog in the world. I can appreciate many people are biased towards thinking that their dog is adorable, but nobody compares to little Bobby. A stunning cavalier King Charles spaniel. He's white and auburn (like his older brother, me) with a perfect auburn spot on the top of his head. We're not one of those families who made an Instagram account for our dog because we aren't moronic, but if we had, he'd probably have more followers than Cristiano Ronaldo.

He's a real heartthrob around the park; he has all the other dogs he encounters on a piece of string, bowing before his tiny frame and playing to his promiscuous tune. This is an issue as my dad refused to have him neutered, comparing it to not having me or my younger brother castrated (unsure if the comparison is valid but that's the level of treatment our young prince has). Another fine example of professional people thinking they know everything (i.e. my dad thinking he knew what's best for the dog as opposed to a vet giving him expert advice). Unfortunately, with all the submissive canines bowing before him, it results in Bobby trying to mount any and every dog he engages with – male or female, cross or pure breed, ugly or not – he does not discriminate, I'm not sure how age works in the world of dogs but there doesn't seem to be any screening process from Bobby. Nor does he ever successfully penetrate (thankfully); he's too small. He just stands on his hind legs with his front paws up and humps, more often than not, thin air. I wonder where he's learned that trick. He thinks he's a tiny porn star. If we'd have known his libido was so incredibly high, we would have given him a more suitable porn star name like Bobby Rocket or Teddy Casio, something like that. He's always up for it (yes, literally, well done), but never quite gets there because he's so small (and again).

There is no relationship in the world like a family and their dog have; nothing can compare. They unite us just by being there, they cheer us up through any times of sorrow, and they cuddle up to us as much as possible; they're such loving creatures. They're most likely so fond of us because we give them treats and think they can do no wrong. Realistically, if I cocked my leg against the sofa and urinated because I hadn't been outside for an hour and just wagged my backside when I was questioned about it, my mum would grab me by the scruff of the neck and try to stick my nose in it. She'd probably succeed as well before volleying me up and down the house.

The beauty about being away from home is the excitement of knowing I'll be returning for a long weekend. It's the delight of knowing Bobby will be around me every minute I'm in the house, he'll be sniffing around and rubbing his head into my legs. And, returning to my overwhelmingly loud family never gets old. They treat me like the prodigal son every couple of months when I return. I unashamedly play up to it as well, for I deserve to be treated like a prince, especially as my sister is undoubtedly my parents' favourite most of the time. The enjoyment of returning somewhere I am loved, acknowledged and people care about me (for a few minutes at least) after having spent months in a shark tank of self-serving individuals, is enough for me. I can go home and be adored. I just love the attention really; I'm needy (if you've not picked up on it). I'm not openly needy however, I just crave it internally. I'd never ask for attention, I just welcome any I receive and make sure it's prolonged as much as possible. I hate sympathy though unless I'm ill; sympathy is for victims.

The reason I adore home so much is that at home I'm reminded of my childhood at every turn. Life as a child is infinitely better than life as an adult; no job, no pointless anxieties and the school day finished at twenty past three. We could run home without a care in the world, eating tonnes of sweets, drinking full-fat Coke and then four rounds of white toast before bed, being completely ignorant of what it could do to our waistlines. No staying late to finish work on behalf of someone we don't know. We could just skip home, play out with friends, or play on the Xbox with them and not be judged for not having a life. As children, we had no fear in the world (fear of the dark excluded). We were free. This is the beauty of childhood, having the feeling of doing whatever we wanted. Even if it was just going on a bike ride round the block (as long as you didn't crash the bike into your auntie's car and it haunt you forevermore).

We didn't know any better because we didn't have to. All the answers we sought we could get from our parents and take their word as the ultimate, even for all the pointless lies they threw our way to get us to do something. "Carrots make you see in the dark." I'd shovel carrots into my mouth by the bunch expecting to turn the light off one evening and have night vision. Didn't quite happen, cheers Mum. "If you eat your crusts your hair goes curly..." I spent my entire youth dodging crusts like bullets and still ended up with a genetic kink in my hair, ginger and curly. I wouldn't wish that on anybody, thanks again Mum. Who invented these myths? Why are they passed down through generations? If I have a kid, they'll be told to eat their vegetables or they'll look like the fat kid in their school. If they want to eat crusts, go for it. They'll probably get the kink in their hair anyway. I just have to hope they aren't ginger as well.

We've all had that moment, however old when we realise that our parents have lied to us all our lives and what for;

some sort of greater good, for our benefit? I'm certain if my mum told me I'd have kids pointing and laughing at me, telling me I've got more rolls on my belly than the bakers, I wouldn't care about night vision. I'd be asking for carrots and greens over smiley faces all day.

Parents then attempt to justify their lies when called out on it; it is totally unacceptable. They're just like politicians and the media outlets trying to cover up scandals of the past. How can we believe anything when we have spent our lives being lied to by those closest to us? My dad still won't admit to me that Santa isn't real. Although I'm slightly more easygoing with that lie. I believe and he still comes every year. So as long as he keeps coming, I'll believe in the fat, jolly fella up in the North Pole. Keep the presents coming, I'm happy with you Santa. World War 3 almost erupted in my house when my mum tried to tell me at the age of 12 that Santa didn't exist. I've never seen my dad so upset with anything other than football. I'm fairly sure it was the closest I've seen my parents come to splitting up. It was carnage. I have no idea what I'd have done. My Christmas list would have been replaced with divorce papers. The only Christmas miracle I could have hoped for would have been night vision from my carrots on Christmas Day because my mum was happy to keep up with that lie; absolute maniac.

Another wonderful thing about home is sitting down to a roast, a proper roast. Sundays were made for snacks, long naps and roasts, not avocado brunches and walks in the park; they can get in the bin. The north-south divide is pretty meaningless to me, though it is bizarre how you're viewed as a different species if you live anywhere north of Watford. Though northern folk arriving south and stating the classic phrase, 'You wouldn't get that up north' at any given opportunity irritates me just as much as southerners mimicking any word somebody with a regional accent says.

Still, if somebody has a coat on in the middle of December, 'You wouldn't get that up north.' You would, mate. Having lived in the North for 21 years of my life, I can confirm people wear coats. It's a massive hoax and contrary to popular belief, coat-wearing exists up and down the country, particularly in times of low temperature. That being said, the one time I notice a distinct divide between north and south is through a Sunday roast. Up north, the Yorkshire pudding is bigger than my face, there's no need for messing around with fancy presentation. All the usual suspects arrive on the plate: meat, carrots, cauliflower cheese, broccoli, mash (if you're feeling funky) and crispy roast potatoes that have been bathed in goose fat. The lot is smothered in gravy and I mean smothered. It was a culinary delight during my youth, even if my mum likes her beef well done (I know). After my first long, wet Sunday in London, I headed out for a pub roast; just what I needed after a winter's day. The sun had set at half four, the rain was crashing down, it was bitterly cold and everyone was wearing coats (which is how I can remember it was my first in London). I sat down with a pint of Coke (ice no lemon, remember, never lemon) and ordered my roast thinking, *here we go, time to see the week off properly*. I rarely rub my hands together with excitement, but when food is imminent I can't control my actions. I like to think I'd rub them looking like a rapper in a music video looking super-cool, so we'll go with that being how I looked even though I was alone in a posh gastro pub and not inside a Rolls Royce filled with cigar smoke, champagne and honeys. It was a stunning modern gastro pub in fairness, situated right on the canal that runs towards east London, a real picturesque setting to watch the rainfall; it felt cool, you know?

I made eye contact with the waiter as he left the kitchen, plate in his hand raised next to his shoulder. I could see the Yorkshire pudding peering over at me. So I slung my napkin over my lap (you wouldn't get that up north, would you?). I feel a unique sense of excitement when eye contact is made with a waiter. I can feel if the plate is mine. When you know, you just know, you know? He skipped over and placed it down in front of me. My goofy grin stretched right across my face as I saw the steam rise from the plate. He took his arm away.

"Enjoy."

Oh thank you my friend, I will. I turned to my plate.

Diabolical. Zero greenery on the plate, the portion was worthy of feeding a ferret and the Yorkshire pudding could have been eaten in one large mouthful. I noticed the gravy was stored in some sort of eggcup and then I saw the beetroot. Hang on, beetroot? I couldn't fathom why I saw beetroot on my plate. I checked the menu again – 'all the trimmings'. I was shocked and not in a fun surprised way. The sadness didn't hit me until I'd finished the meal. It was categorically one of the worst I've ever had in terms of expectation versus delivery, it was almost tormenting. Beetroot on a roast – you wouldn't get that up north (if anyone disagrees and thinks you probably would, that's okay just keep it to yourself).

I can't be too discouraging of London cuisine, it's the most diverse city (have I mentioned that?) in the world and the food is homage to it. I can walk to the end of my street and I'm able to step into a family-owned Vietnamese, an authentic Japanese restaurant, a glorious Italian owned by a man named Antonio, a 'bring your own booze' Indian with the spiciest of traditional menus and the purest of all American restaurants in the world, McDonald's, Mamma Mia. Every corner of every street of every borough in London hosts amazing restaurants and bars: meat-loving, vegan, fresh fish, hipster, high end – it goes on. You could spend a lifetime in the city and never eat at the same place twice. If I'd have stayed at home, the endless possibilities become, well, slightly more finite, particularly when a new burger joint opens in town and the entire city's population goes there every third day for six months and just as they get bored, the next one suddenly opens. It is essentially the same place, only this time, their specialty is halloumi fries instead of sweet potato fries; exciting! I'll stick to my bean and crushed avocado chilli burger, on a gluten-free bun served with a soya strawberry milkshake down here for now.

Living away has made me much fonder of my home. I long to be there, however brief the visit, mainly because at home everything is free. I can drop my clothes anywhere in the house and they'll find their way back to my room, washed, ironed and folded. Living on my own, it is me who has to perform these arduous tasks. During my four years in London, I've lived alone, with a mate and with my girlfriend. Each option brings different positives and negatives and I have a brief guide to each. One thing I am proud to have never done is house share with random people. Life is too short to spend time with people who could potentially kill me in my sleep for the sake of a couple of hundred quid a month (yes, even though it wasn't me paying the rent).

Living alone

Living alone is incredible. I lived without judgement or expectation, other than judgement from friends and family who knew my rent was being subsidised; though I wasn't going to lie and pretend I'd funded a one-bed flat near Hyde Park by myself. I could walk around wearing boxers and a dressing gown (pyjama shorts, but that sounds juvenile so let's pretend they're boxers) without worrying about how badly I smell. I could sit and binge through a Netflix series for eight hours without worrying whether the person I was watching it with was enjoying it or no. It saves the effort of having to look in the direction of the other person to check they're laughing along or are as immersed in the drama as I am despite me having watched it three times over. I didn't have to pick up after anybody but myself. If I made a mess I knew I'd have to deal with it, it was my responsibility (if only everybody in the world acted upon the same principles). I knew if I had crumbs all over myself and the sofa it was upon me to brush them off and hoover up anything around it; to preserve the well-being of the flat for any future habitants (see what I'm getting at?). Living alone is like being in a perfect cocoon. I didn't want to be a beautiful butterfly and flap my wings to cause a hurricane, no thank you world. I was at peace in my little shell.

Meal times and food shops were without quarrel about who fancies what for dinner that week. Nobody moans, claiming not to like spicy food so we have to settle for a korma over something with a little more kick when we make a curry (call me exotic, I know). Catering to one's own need is much simpler; thinking about the needs of others is so tiring, time-consuming and, often expensive. Living alone allowed me to freely not care about the welfare of others. I didn't have to worry about the way anybody else felt. I didn't have to cater for other tastes. This was a perfectly acceptable attitude to have in my flat. Of course, I'm not so selfish outside of it. I wait for a world where people aren't as self-serving and treat others with great empathy, making sure everybody is fed. There's no ambiguity on portion sizes or who gets what. A world where everybody is completely understanding and conscious that everyone must get a fair share. Wouldn't it be great?

This is why living alone was so magnificent. I was allowed, for once, to be selfish, to be careless; all about me. Unlike out there with all the sharing and compromising with other people. Being selfish is so much more straightforward, often beneficial as well. Sometimes I think I should try it more and be adventurous with my greed.

Sadly there are a couple of disadvantages to living alone. Most importantly, the fear of the dark as night descends. Every groan, creak, or bang was amplified when I was alone. There was nobody to turn to for reassurance that it was merely a window closing in the distance, or just the wind. Instead, I used to sit up with the television on, trying to distract myself from waiting for my flat to be invaded by a supernatural being that would then slaughter me without a fair trial. There's no hiding when alone; no one to protect us. If somebody comes, they're coming solely for the person inside. If that's you, well, good night.

In addition to the fear is the amount of overthinking when alone every day. As humans, being inside our own head for our entire waking time is among the biggest agony we can experience (excluding genuine agonies: war, death, famine, prejudice, etc.). We sit and fret over a never-ending catalogue of issues in our lives until we arrive deep inside the pit of our own memory, tormenting ourselves over the singular tortilla crisp we pinched from the salad bar in Tesco when we were seven and how if that ever surfaces, we're finished. We're still good people, aren't we? Of course we are, but we need reassurance to avoid the feeling of shame and self-loathing that often follows these intense, crippling periods of thought. If you're living alone, you need to keep yourself occupied, or you will go completely mad. Even masturbation gets boring (that's the only lie in the book).

Despite the dark feelings of fright and loneliness, the freedom of living alone is incomparable and completely outweighs the downside; if you can make it through the night. Fundamentally, we want to be free. Being in our own space where nobody can enter, we can sing along to our guilty pleasures in the mirror for half an hour, dance without being seen, or even just poo with the door open. It is a perfect space to be in, just as long as you can enjoy your own company. If not then you need a flatmate.

Flatmate

Living with my mate was everything I imagined it would be. My friend and I decided to move in together after he finished his Masters degree and moved back down south. He needs no introduction other than he is Ashton Kutcher from *That '70s Show*, or thinks he is. We can refer to him as Ingo. We decided that when living together we would break the graduate stereotype, so found a flat not far from Clapham North station (in the south of London, where about 90% of graduate scheme occupants live). The first couple of weeks were ruthless, we were out constantly. It was like the first night of a sixth-form holiday (lads, lads, lads), every night. Doesn't get more Ayia-fucking-Napa than me throwing up over the balcony on our first night onto the balcony below. Though admittedly I didn't feel too rebellious when I went down with a bucket and sponge to clean it up the next day. I blamed it on someone else but took responsibility as the occupant of the flat. They gave me their number and said we should sort drinks one time; we never did. I'm an embarrassment.

If we stayed in, we'd sit up until the early hours covering every topic possible, from football to politics to religion (yawn) and eventually to deep, meaningful questions, such as, what would your everyday superpower be? If anyone is wondering, it came down to either the ability to never spill food or drink on my clothes, or have the ability to iron any item of clothing just by putting it on. There are many fantastic everyday superpowers out there, it's important to find the one that suits your less supernatural needs (perhaps you wish to stop crying into your pillow after masturbating).

Food for thought, anyway. When we would hit the cut-off point of 'we need to go to bed now to get our six hours of sleep', we'd be incredibly upset as we forcibly said goodnight for the next six hours. Living with a true friend is like any dramatic depiction or sitcom. Even sitting in and doing nothing is such fun because we could sit there and talk the most senseless tripe in our pyjama shorts (probably weird if I called them boxers here) and t-shirts. Dreamland.

If you don't live in pyjamas you're living a lie.

There was a long honeymoon period for both of us. It drained me physically, emotionally and worst of all, financially. Going out was a given; trips to The Falcon pub became too frequent. Then one day, the honeymoon period flickered away, work fatigue had settled in and someone (me) had started to show their short temper. It became a test of our relationship. The utmost important factor for a housemate is matching levels of cleanliness. Some fraudsters out there pretend to be 'relatively okay' when it comes to cleaning because they plugged a hoover in twice a year in their student accommodation or put the dishwasher on twice a week. This wasn't student accommodation; this was the big time. It's critical to find a companion who at least makes an effort to match your own level of house maintenance. If you're lazy, match yourself with someone lazy, coexist in your pigsty together. You deserve to fester in a grotty bin. If you're a normal human being who knows how to make their own bed, hoover and clean up after meal times, find someone who'll match that effort; it's all we deserve. Standards never slip. Even better, find someone willing to pay for a cleaner, that's the pinnacle. Though at the age of 22 it was probably less likely to find someone willing to pay for a cleaner than me finding myself in a bed with both Blake Lively and Ryan Reynolds.

Living with a friend is how I think marriage would be –

there's always going to be bickering, pointless arguments, and neither person reacts to the other being naked (not even a flinch). At least we had separate bathrooms. He's one of those handsome people who had a full beard at 22, which looked great but he'd shave it with a beard trimmer and his little face pubes would scatter everywhere, too far for him to clear up. So there would just be dead beard all around the sink unit. I think I went in his bathroom twice and didn't last long either time.

(I still can't grow a beard.)

Through the countless nights out, ventures in The Falcon (what a pub), substandard meals and arguments over whose turn it was to head to the supermarket, there were a handful of moments that defined our relationship as housemates. These moments were from the less glamorous times, like steam-cleaning the floor the night after a flat party, both having to scrape chewing gum off the floor with a knife despite the most unforgiving hangovers making us want to catch a one-way flight to Switzerland. Reflecting on hardship is something we're most talented at in this country. We love talking about our previous struggles as if we ever have endured a meaningful one. I'm talking about scraping several pieces of chewing gum off a floor like it's an actual hardship while there's still widespread racism in this country – from disproportionate stopping and searching, to racist abuse online going unpunished, to complete lack of representation in management roles across all sectors. Before you roll your eyes, according to the *Independent* newspaper at the time of writing this, there were more FTSE100 white CEOs called Steve than all FTSE100 CEOs from ethnic minority backgrounds. That's a bit crazy.

We're in our element as we tell the tormenting tales of evil that we have overcome, particularly when we have shared such a moment with somebody else. Whether it's attention or empathy we're craving, we do our best to attract both as much as possible. There's always one story above all, a 'that time when' story to trump all others. The story that glues friends together, binding their souls forevermore. I'll never forget ours, one night in Clapham.

Unfortunately for me, every night I am in bed, my mind plays tricks on me (as established with me living alone). I get into bed and in the silence of the night, my mind asks itself, *What is your deepest fear? If you were to wake up in the night in a cold alarming sweat, what would be standing over your body as you squirm and squeal, begging for it to stop?* The short answer to mine is anything and everything. If I wake up in the middle of the night, I believe the silence alone could kill me; I'm that much of a wimp. I'm unaware as to why I'm so cursed by the terrors of the night, but it's something I live with, alone or with others.

There was one night in Clapham that the terror was more than my wild imagination. I bolted up in the darkness as usual, eyes on stalks, ears at highest alert and, my senses in overdrive, reacting to anything. *You're just imagining things,* I told myself. I'd probably just woken from a really cool dream but felt nothing, as I was so preoccupied. It was a rude awakening, one where my stomach was cramped, feeling like someone was clenching a fist inside it. Fearing that if I didn't move, my water would break and I'd give birth, I rolled out of bed and made my way across the bedroom and into the bathroom. (Obviously, I had the en suite room because I'm such a prima donna.)

I was scrambling around in the dark, blindly aiming for the toilet. I felt like a drunk American wielding a gun, blindfolded being asked to shoot the apple off someone's head from 100 yards. It was complete guesswork. I had to aim for the water and use the sound of trickling to know I wasn't urinating all over my own floor (life is like pissing in the dark, remember). I slowly released and waited for the reassuring splashing sound, once it came through I could relax. Only the glare of the TV in the mirror provided a flicker of light in the darkened en suite. I was itching to get back to bed, willing my bladder to empty itself. Then I heard a peculiar scratching noise. Being on red alert, the scratch was so loud it sounded as if it were inside my skull. I turned my head, aware that I couldn't move my body without decorating the bathroom wall. I was caught with my trousers down. I hurried to finish, dribbling into my pants: no time to shake it off like Taylor Swift told us. Good job I only wear black shorts. I felt for the tap above the sink. I fiddled and rinsed in a flash, wiping my hands down my (already wet) pyjama shorts as I rushed back to bed to base myself and listen.

The television screen illuminated the room, but the sound was completely down. I waited in the silence, sitting upright in bed. A scraping sound to the back right of the bed pulled my attention. I leapt toward the right-hand pillow: nothing. Another scrape came from the other side of the bed. This was like a horror film. I army-rolled across my bed and hung my head over the left-hand pillow to peer down and search for an explanation for the mysterious scratching. I couldn't see a thing. Then I looked to my right, towards the foot of the bed.

The beige carpet was shining under the glare of the television and across the bright surface scurried a small dark figure at lightning pace towards a bag in the corner of the room. It was too quick for me to fixate my eyes on it but I knew I was not alone. I went completely stiff with fear. I would not be getting back to sleep as soon as I thought. Adrenaline began to surge through my body; it was fight or flight and I wanted to go with the latter. I was curious as to what beast had joined me in my room, praying it wasn't a goliath spider, as a spider that big would have been searching for a pair of my shoes to put on. Please, not a spider. I edged towards the foot of the bed, reaching for my bag, slowly. My heart was pounding to the point I felt sick. Ready, set, lift, and the blurred figure darted beneath the bed once again. I nearly hit the ceiling, before crashing against the headboard of the bed and flicking the lamp switch. I let out a yelp. It was now about survival.

"Wake up, I need you in here," I sounded the alarm.

After several seconds of shuffling about, I heard a groan from his room.

"Please, there's something in my room and it is*big!*"

I couldn't be alone in this cell any longer. The walls had closed in and the space between the beast and me became tighter with each passing second. I was choking on my own breath; why can't I have a fondness for small animals like I do for dogs? Anything with more than four legs is an obscurity that I cannot understand and will not face under any circumstance, particularly in my bedroom in the middle of the night.

The door creaked open, we'd only said goodbye hours ago, but I'd never been so happy to see my flatmate; my knight bursting through the door to my aid. I wasn't facing this bout alone. We were in it together from now on. We searched for the creature ruffling around under the bed. It was almost as if it had vanished into thin air. Until, out of the corner of my eye, nestled in a crevice between the bedside table and the wardrobe, tucked away in the back right corner, I spied a mouse. It wasn't particularly intimidating when stood still; seeming to be in shock of the situation it had found itself in. It stared at two growing boys in their early twenties looking back at it, scratching their heads and talking gibberish with the occasional point in its direction. We were plotting on how to capture the pesky bugger. If anyone has seen Tom and Jerry, you'd know these creatures are cunning and quick. Between my engineer flatmate and myself, surely we could lure a mouse into a trap and set it free elsewhere (or kill it with a heavy blunt object and not tell anyone). We rubbed our heads together over the best way of luring it out from the corner so we could place a box over it, remove it from the flat and set it free without injuring it (I'm not a psychopath). If it came to injuring it, of course, we would have to. There was no competition between the mouse and us as it approached four in the morning.

Using the experience we had and the lessons we'd learned from years of television, we went to lure the mouse onto the lid of a plastic box, using grated cheddar. I can now confirm from that evening that mice are not remotely interested in mature cheddar. The staring competition endured for 15 minutes, until, like the brave knight he was, my flatmate made a suicidal beeline for the mouse, trying to flick it out of the corner with his finger. The mouse scarpered out across the room and we both jumped onto the bed, shrieking so the whole of south London could hear us. Pandemonium ensued, which ended with us cowering away from a mouse no bigger than a pebble. I didn't know fear until the fear that struck with a rodent invasion. Among the commotion, the mouse disappeared into the night, knowing it could never return.

To this day, I have no idea on the final destination of the old bean; it played its cards well. It was in and out within 20 minutes (that I know of) and it caused maximum distress and damage for the occupants of the flat (a broken lamp and some wasted cheese). We agreed to discuss the mouse tale only when absolutely necessary, which is why I've chosen it now.

Living with a mate is a challenge, but it is an unbelievable ride. Through the hardship and the squabbling, there are stories that last a lifetime (probably more fun than the mouse story but I felt it defined our living relationship), laughs that do not tire and memories that cement a little mark in each other's lives. I was fortunate enough to live with a friend I could drive mad but still go for drinks a couple of times a week with. It's completely worth any difficulty for the stories that come through on the other side. Cheers to you, Ingo.

Though having said that, he got so fed up with me, he moved to the Middle East for a break from both tax authorities and me. I know for a fact he was more excited to get away from me than Her Majesty's Revenue and Customs for a couple of years; make it rain big man.

Dr Girlfriend flatmate

Having lived with her for almost two years, I feel I'm now heading to my final resting place. This isn't intended to sound romantic in any way; I believe this is the end of me. There are two fundamentals to this theory: firstly, she is a doctor (specifically a GP trainee); secondly, she's almost four years older than me.

I know.

Let's get up to speed. Many who've been through the entirety of university as a single person will know of the final term love scramble. This is when people realise there won't be a better chance to meet a life companion after leaving university, so try to spark some sort of meaningful relationship to take into the real world. I entered my final term with nothing but the hope of establishing some contact with the only person I was interested in, if not, then it was time to enter the realm of online dating and begin an uphill struggle. I couldn't face telling my children that their mother and I met by mutually swiping right on an app to approve of each other's aesthetics (I know it's a common way to meet nowadays, don't worry). I have lived a sheltered life in fairness to any love app love finders. In the first week of my last term (notice the use of the word 'term' over 'semester'), I began speaking to the girl whom I'd been shamelessly attempting to get to know (not sure how else to label it – get with/date/marry/call it what you want) for the best part of two and a half years. By 'speaking to' I mean I'd bump into her on nights out when we were both too drunk to formulate a meaningful conversation but I'd still offer her a drink, before finding myself alone stumbling to the local curry house for the full works at four in the morning.

One morning early on in our final year, I woke up with her contact details in my phone, only to realise I'd rang her twice at about five. This somehow didn't scare her away forever. I'd had shoulder surgery and my arm was in a sling. She said she'd take my stitches out if I needed her to, so gave me her number; she denies it to this day but that is what happened. The first night out of the final term is when our 21st-century love story began. From there, we casually dated and the medical professional-to-be somehow enjoyed our few dates as much as me (this isn't a romantic novel as I won't go into details but our first date involved drinks and pizza; easy). Either that, or her levels of desperation were too much for her. After graduation, we leapt into my first relationship since my school days. It was exhilarating. I was infatuated with her. I felt like I was with a pop star, but an older pop star, like Cher or Whitney. I'd never felt cool, but this was probably the closest I was to feeling it.

After both spending two years in London (I was meant to do a Masters degree in Sheffield but didn't achieve a high enough grade in my degree, so moved to London for work and to follow her, but refuse to admit it to her), we felt it was time to move in together. Well, she felt that we should move in together as she approached 27, wanting security, responsibility and commitment. I was approaching 23 and had barely discovered armpit hair, so to say our interests were misaligned is an understatement. Naturally, within 12 months of her suggesting we take the next step in our relationship, I'd agreed to plunge with both feet (like the coward I am). I think moving in with partners, much like marriage, is something that people jump into a little too quickly for my liking. I've done farts that have lasted longer than some marriages. Like when people meet on TV shows and move in together eight weeks after crossing paths, then wonder why it doesn't work out after the public has stopped caring about them. It's probably because the next show has aired and they've been forgotten; other than the occasional Instagram post of some next-generation protein powder or luxury underwear line from a budget designer in Norwich.

Moving in needs to feel natural and the relationship has to have been tested. Having been with her for two years, Dr Girlfriend and I were at the point where we could have debates without her thinking we were on the brink of being over forever. I still get scared she'll finish me, or she could look at me in the shower after I'd just been on a run and laugh at my penis. True story; it hurt. I'm not sure it was even cold that day. Ultimately, I knew we'd get on because that's meant to be the reason people enter relationships, isn't it? We are meant to enjoy each other's company, be it naked or not. I (she) thought we should move in together as it was natural, I (she) thought it felt right. I (didn't but had no choice) agreed to it, not because I wanted to but because I had to or she'd have left me, so it felt natural to do so. I knew from that point how my life would be from then on; living in fear, afraid to speak my mind, forevermore. There we have it.

True love.

Her occupation (I'm going to try my best and not use the word doctor) has quite an impact on our living arrangements and dynamics of our relationship. This has included me being woken up at half five every morning (I don't care how many times she argued her case, it's very annoying being woken up at half five when you don't need to be up until two hours later; my alarm is bad enough) for six months because her rotation required her to be in work at seven to see screaming babies emerge from badly torn vaginas. Over time, I've become immune to being put off my food. I'm now able to eat a beef ragu while discussing stage four tears, anal prolapses and fungal diseases in and around sexual organs.

Yeasty.

(No I don't know what any of the above actually means.)

In most relationships, when one of the coupled (or more) parties are of ill health, the other(s) offer sympathy, be at their side, serve soup and hot drinks on demand and, tend to any need. They'd also ensure their companion was wrapped up, repeatedly tucking in to ensure warmth and will their compatriot on the road to being cured. Living with a doctor (sorry), however, not a chance. I'm unsure whether it's from the winding-up she receives from the moronic patients who've arrived in the A&E department with a blister or concerned by their body odour; or the fact she's lost the will with people who have come to her having taken three pills at once instead of three pills across 12 hours asking for medical advice; or perhaps she's grown tired from situations like when she had sewn a patient's throat back together, only for the patient to go the toilet, take a razor blade from their underwear and slit it back open. As a side note, I'm sure her book would be far more interesting than mine (after reading a draft of this, a friend recommended the works of Adam Kay for a similar insight; I read it while editing this book and thoroughly enjoyed it, doctors really do deserve better). Though I couldn't be a doctor for so many reasons, mainly I'm not clever enough; despite my ongoing medical degree. Whatever broke her spirit, it means I get no sympathy or attention when sick, at all. The key issue is she'll know exactly what's up with me, which is usually nothing more than me wanting attention and she will offer me nothing but a routine, "Come on, you're okay." Rubbish.

That being said, having been diagnosed with Crohn's Disease means I get occasional sympathy (even though she thinks it was either a misdiagnosis or an incredibly mild form). But even then it takes cameras being thrust down my throat or propelled up my backside for her to acknowledge that I'm remotely unwell. The old double camera penetration is a mortifying experience I wouldn't wish on anybody. My first ever took place in a hospital (as you'd expect) in west London; it's too awful to not share. If you are squeamish, feel free to skip to 'Living through glass' because this isn't for you. (I know you're going to read it, but don't say I didn't warn you.)

I'd been through the standard procedure of a 24-hour starvation together with the solution taken to flush my system out. I'd put the hard work in and arrived at the hospital a little twitchy for my first time on camera. The consultant manning the helm of this procedure visited me in the waiting room and ran through the process of the dual camera operation. One gastroscopy, where a camera would be inserted down my numbed throat to examine my stomach and one colonoscopy, with the other camera veering up my back passage to check my bowel and it would all be on screen for me to see. Front row view of my own innards; nothing to worry about. The stage was set. I was stripped down and covered with a modesty robe, and wearing mesh underwear in case I lost control of my near-empty bowels. Feeling optimistic (and being naïve), I hopped on the bed and was all smiles with the middle-aged consultant, who I could tell had seen it all before. Just as I began to relax, two young female nurses of a similar age to myself entered the room.

"Morning Andrew," the first one said.

I returned the pleasantries hastily, bewildered by why they were in the room with me. I thought perhaps they were just checking I could tell them my name and address, or ensuring I was having the correct anaesthetic and they weren't going to send me under for eight hours by mistake. They began to make preparations for the procedure with the consultant, which involved gloving up and I quickly realised this was an ambush. These ladies were going nowhere.

I didn't panic at the first camera as it came straight for my throat, I was too busy fretting about what was to follow, where my backside would be in the air facing towards these young innocent nurses with a lengthy tube being relentlessly shoved into it. I began convincing myself this was a routine procedure; probably their third of the day given it was late morning. This was nothing out of the ordinary for the medical staff. For me, it was unchartered territory and these waters were not kind. My face warmed with embarrassment at the thought of my bum exposure.

"Open wide please," the other requested in a sweet yet forceful manner as she sprayed a lovely banana flavour into my mouth also known as magic numbing spray to medical professionals.

What I heard was, "This is it kid, no going back now."

The consultant prepared the oral insertion. I knew at this point I could only comply and hope for the best; I told myself I would never see these people again and reassured myself that it couldn't go too badly, could it?

The gastroscopy lasted just a few minutes. It may have been short but it was certainly not sweet. I continuously gagged and my eyes streamed as the camera was plunged down my throat and into my stomach. My mouth was completely numb but my chest and stomach twitched as the device clattered around my insides. The sedatives battled to numb the pain but the process still crippled me. My eyes wept the entire time. The relief of the camera being reeled from my stomach was like coming up for air for the first time after almost drowning. I gasped for air but had to make out that I was unscathed to the surrounding health staff. I didn't want them to think I was a baby.

Part one over, but the worst was still to come (and it would be so much worse). Health professionals are modest individuals, particularly during sensitive times, but I am not. Like most, I find being naked in front of strangers an awkward affair, particularly when being probed while sedated. I couldn't imagine what it must be like to be a ketamine-filled tiger being prodded to pose for photos with people wanting to show their love for wild animals (the coolest kind of people).

Following my coughing and splurging from part one, the nurses rolled me onto my side, exposing the back of my pale body to the room. I lay helplessly on my side. It was so cold it caused my testicles to tingle. Thankfully my front was covered up (I think it was anyway). Not that there's a chance they'd have been peeking had it not been. I waited like an animal in a slaughterhouse, powerless, motionless, and wishing it would be over in a split second. Despite the warning, I jerked as the consultant lubricated my backside with a cold viscous paste. The cold came as a slight shock to my sedated system, but it could not compare to the surprise that would follow. This was the closest I'd relate to being a ketamine-fuelled animal. I was spaced out, but aware of everything, I just couldn't do anything. The screen adjacent to the hospital bed caught my eye as the camera link activated. The screen now showed the hospital floor as the tube hung from the machine it was attached to. I watched on as the camera began to move. I was amazed by the fact the hospital room was onscreen. I smiled at the tour of the room I was getting on the television, which I now know is a distraction technique used by the doctor. I could only half-raise my arm at the screen because I was limp through the sedative, but I pointed and slurred the words, "I'm on TV." I can't believe I said, "I'm on TV." Hi Mum, by the way.

The camera then locked onto its target. The screen showed the back of my body and eventually my pale backside, which was primed and ready for insertion. The smile disappeared; I didn't want to be on TV anymore. Unless you work in pornography, you are never going to see your arse bent over and primed for insertion like the view I had. I wish I could have taken a picture but I'm not sure that request would go down well (nor was I thinking about it at the time). I realised I don't have a bum for porn. I saw it so up close, I could see my own goosebumps. They really should have had the heating on.

By the way, where did all the hair come from?

To enable the camera to access the body, air is fired up the anus to generate space for the camera to manoeuvre without causing damage to the poor subject (me). The initial entrance of the camera made my pelvis thrust forward through instinct. It was simply a phenomenon I was not accustomed to (incidentally it didn't hurt like I thought it would). As the camera began to coil through my insides, my intestines felt like they'd caught fire. Despite the painkillers, I was groaning from the pain I felt inside. The dosage of sedative was increased to ease the discomfort but to no avail; the worst was still to come. I did my best to keep still; to stop myself writhing from the pain caused inside as moving only worsened it. My self-awareness disappeared and I began moaning like a cow giving birth. Was there a baby cow in there?

After an unbearably long period of stomach cramps, whaling and my insides throbbing, the camera was hoisted out (talk about relief). I was incapable of controlling my body as the long tube (it was so long) made its final exit from the depths of, well, me. All the air which had been inserted for the camera fired out after it. It was like an enormous unknotted balloon being released in west London. The combination of length and volume was astounding. I was like a brass band reaching a crescendo, with the note being held forever. The release from my slab of a body felt so tremendous it was breathtaking, until I realised there was an audience to my little brass ensemble (would woodwind be more appropriate?). I'd just emptied roughly 40 minutes of pressurised air into a small room with three or four other people. I was too far under to think about the smell. I could only bury my head in the pillow, keep my head down and hope everybody would go away. I fell asleep following the big bang and the invisible mushroom cloud dispersed through the hospital while I lay unconscious.

I woke up two hours later to a lovely blonde doctor four years my senior at my side, having arrived from her night shift at her hospital.

"Come on, you're okay, big baby," was the first thing she said to me.

Big baby? She's lucky she was clutching a McDonald's breakfast for two, or I'd have shown her big baby. At least she was unaware of the quarantine incident just hours earlier. I slowly returned to normality and upon the news of my awakening, the consultant returned, telling me that the pain I felt was roughly one-tenth of what a woman in labour experiences; and that's how I became a feminist.

It seems these are the lengths I must go to get my companion's attention and receive sympathy; alas no. The only other positive from that day is little else can embarrass me in this world thanks to my flawless A-major symphony performance in room C.12; cheers to that. If only I'd taken photos of myself on the hospital bed looking a little worse for wear, thanking the hospital for all they've done, I could generate mass sympathy on social media to make me feel better; perhaps it was a missed opportunity. The McDonald's breakfast and returning to my flat for a couple of days off work sufficed. Besides, I'm not sure I could thank the hospital that day for the pain they put me through, though it was an eye [among other parts]-opener. I've had the procedure twice more since and almost look forward to it now, like a little holiday, where I'm free of my ego, free from any meaningless worries, and most importantly, free from my phone. I'm not sure bum-selfies (or bumfies as I'm going to call them) are going to trend anytime soon, not from that angle. Not mine anyway.

This was my (not so) quick guide to living alone, with a friend and with my doctor girlfriend (whom I adore, obviously). Though these concepts are hardly unheard of, I've tried to discuss the fundamentals of my living situations without acknowledging another huge part about how I (and millions of others) now live. The experiences of our generation differ so much from any generation before because it is never just us. Without sounding like a conspiracy theorist, we now live together in the little toxic world of social media and beyond. We no longer live behind closed doors. Technology has invaded and is here to stay in the virtual kingdom we've built for it at the cost of our privacy.

It's time to leap between the physical and the virtual.

Chapter V – The new ordinary

Living through glass

Who'd have known so many people would get such pleasure from four (or so) inches? In the last decade, phones have integrated into our lives, beginning as a nice-to-have gadget and evolving into part of our identity. We no longer just live with those we share a space with; we now live with a huge community, all day, every day. I couldn't write about living, or any routine, without discussing my three-plus hours of screen time per day (as if I needed to know statistically how bad my addiction is). Not only do we carry them on our person at all times, but we also live our lives through them. Any fact, any figure, any piece of literature ever published is just a few clicks away; food is delivered to us with a few taps of the screen and taxis are ordered to our door in three taps (providing they don't cancel after making you wait for ten minutes, with no repercussions for the driver while you're late for your meal as a result). The list goes on. I'll refrain from further listing the overabundance of opportunities we have when clutching our phones, as I'm sure there are more apps than there are words in this book. The point is we can do anything and we do everything with our phones because above all else, phones make our lives much easier. Plus, pornography has never been so easily accessible. What's not to love?

There are however, physical dangers of using phones. Unfortunately, phone screens are not like television screens inside car dashboards; they can't detect when the controller of the vehicle is moving and needs to be paying attention to their surroundings. There's little warning telling people to look ahead instead of hunching over their phone and losing sight of what's going on. People have become so invested in the screen in front of their faces, they'll walk into lampposts (I've done that), or huge road works signs on the way to a football match (guess who), or even oncoming traffic (thankfully no, not me). Most annoyingly, people tend to walk into those who are sensibly walking around without their phone out. Too many times have I experienced some moron storming in my direction looking down into their device, charging at me like a bull to a red rag. Yet I'm unable to move out of the way unless I fancy eating a car windshield. They continue to march on up until the last second when their focus is broken at the sight of feet, they become startled and without an apology they'll shuffle around me, carrying on with their heads buried in the sand. Are phone lanes a real thing?

Using our phones in public can also lead to other dangers. None more so than when using our phones innocently, but the angle at which we hold the phone can be misconstrued and, on occasion, aggressive bystanders can be convinced that we're taking photos of them. People seem to forget that the average person (including themselves) is pretty awful to look at, therefore, why would we want photos of them? I say this is a danger because I was unfortunate enough to find myself in such a situation, inside a bar in Green Park (cultured). To be more precise, it was the toilet of a bar and by bar, I mean a typical London boozer. It was filled with the Thursday night geezers wearing pinstriped suits draped over their shoulders, thinning hairlines, loose wedding rings (to slip off at a moment's notice for a quick game of 'Don't tell my wife') and all the bad baggage you'd expect them to bring.

While I waited for my third taxi of the evening (this not

unusual; obviously ordered through my magnificent phone),
I dashed to the toilet, clutching my work bag to make sure I
didn't feel like I was going to wet myself as soon as I sat in
the taxi (always happens, every time I have more than one
drink). Mid-flow I pinched my phone from my jacket pocket
and checked on the location of my taxi, happily watching the
tiny map of London on my screen as cars whizzed around
in real-time, though my car seemed to just spin on the same
spot for 30 seconds. *Two minutes, lovely*, perfect timing I
thought; finish off, hand wash and out. Though it was a rough
bar, I was still standing in Green Park, so they had warm
water and posh soap, something I fully intended on making
the most of (I do enjoy an elongated hand wash). When out
of nowhere...

"What the fuck are you doing, ay?"

It came from an east London accent and it sounded
aggressive. I looked up from the little city on my screen to the
middle-aged man to my left, who seemed to have a little bee
in his bonnet behind his reddened nose and cheeks. I didn't
know him, but I knew the years of drinking hadn't been kind.
He also reeked of ale.

"What do you mean?" I answered his question with my
own question, which to an impatient Londoner is probably
a wind up.

"You're taking pictures of my cock, you tart!"

At this point, I was still mid-flow but could feel the end
was nigh. As it was a drunk wee it dragged out for a little
longer than usual, so I had no choice but to stay calm and
cool in the situation. I'd locked my phone and while asking
what he meant rather innocently, I put my phone in my
pocket. This is one of the few times in my life that I've been
speechless. I'd like to say I was unable to speak from being
completely baffled as to why he thought I'd take a photo of his
no-doubt wrinkly untouched prune, but it was the fear that

made me silent, in all honesty. I was holding my penis, mid-wee with a drunkard wanting to throw hands (which hadn't been washed). I was a 21-year-old boy, alone in London. This guy looked like he drank six cans of Stella (nothing against Stella) for breakfast on a Saturday before going into the local forest to scrap with the lads. Fun.

He shoved me with his right hand just as I was finishing and about to shake off (always important, Florence and the Machine wrote a song about it). I shifted to the right but managed to aim the dribble into the designated urinal safely and away from my shoes. However, after the moment of penis-aiming precision, I felt the zip of my suit trousers catch myself as I'd shifted weight to my right leg to avoid falling into another bystander. I bit down hard on my lip and winced (not because I could hear 'Mr Brightside' playing, but because my actual penis was injured). I shook it off, shook it off (sorry Florence, or is that Taylor?), through the pain and zipped up in a flash. I noticed at this point he hadn't moved from the urinal, he was still going. Trapped, the hunter had now become the hunted.

I made my way over to the sink, eyes transfixed on the back of his head as he turned side to side in an attempt to get me in his eye line. The soap so fragrant and the water so warm, but I could not enjoy a long washing of my hands, not if I wanted to get away from this cowboy. I grabbed a paper towel and darted towards the door, where finally, I shouted,

"Why would I take a picture of that maggot?" and I bolted upstairs to the sweet sound of, "You little cunt."

I was out of that bar before he'd even thought about shaking. He was fuming but was miles away. I almost feel bad, who knows who he'd have taken his anger out on? All I could think of was the relief I felt in knowing I would live to fight (or dodge one) another day. I'm unsure why people think the world revolves around them and others would spend their time taking pictures of them urinating for no reason. Really? Through human stupidity and paranoia, phones are now a genuine safety hazard and a potential cause for violence.

The Obsession

We now live in a society where we all obsess over our phones. It's at the point where sending messages has become preferable to engaging in conversation (though it is much more fun not having to talk). People live through their phones and in particular social media. I won't pretend to be any different; I'm not that sanctimonious. I'm hyper-conscious about the addiction I have and everybody else has, hence I make an effort to ignore it as much as possible, but consciously ignoring something is what makes me feel like an addict. I have to resist looking at my phone, or if I pick it up through habit I must throw it to the other side of the room (providing a soft and safe landing of course) to prevent me numbing my brain to its hypnotics. I've already confessed to interacting with my phone before I talk to the person I sleep next to, albeit just to press snooze on the alarm button to avoid a brain haemorrhage (and for those glorious nine minutes longer in bed). It's the insignificant interactions as such that feed the addiction. Most of us would say we aren't addicted, much like alcoholics or substance addicts struggle to admit they have an addiction. Is it an addiction when the phone has become such a vital part of our lives? We're all affected in the same way.

The geniuses behind the phone evolution probably thought phones would shape the way we communicate, how we live and operate for the better, but like all technology (excluding AI, for now), the devices are only as successful as the user allows them to be. Phones were designed to be user-friendly enough for almost all human beings to use. What these brilliant minds could not fathom with their creation was how stupid most human beings are, me included. We're habitual, selfish, arrogant, and easily addicted. Always wanting more attention, please. Social media has given everybody a voice that can be heard. Until social media, people would have to become influential to exchange words with a member of the government, a musician, a film star, or a professional athlete. Now it's as easy as typing a message, tagging their profile, and pressing 'send'. Giving everyone this voice, in theory, is magical. It crafts a society where we can see how people of other backgrounds and professions live, having the opportunity to speak to our heroes and people pursuing change. Unfortunately, many use this opportunity to berate people of influence, sometimes to the point where victims of such abuse will have to delete their accounts, or worse, due to being bullied. Nobody thinks. People vent their frustrations in the direction of those better known in society and they channel anger into a message so harsh it is heard. People would rather be known for their hideous bile than not be known at all.

It is objectified stupidity.

Objectified stupidity, did I invent a phrase?

Why people feel the need to publicly vent their feelings online is beyond me. Full-grown adults will sit down and take the time to hammer their feelings into a keyboard to produce a pint-sized rant and spread it virtually to all their followers and potentially more. Step back and think about what they're doing. Could you imagine somebody calling their friends and family to a hall to listen as said-person stands on a table and shouts, (I say shouts because it tends to be typed in capital letters), about how their newly ex-partner had cheated with their best friend from school, holding up pictures as well? Would we want to attend the hall meeting? Probably yes, in theory. However, if an invite came in the post to attend on a

Thursday evening, I'd imagine the audience wouldn't be too large. Take me to a bar with Monty Montague and the lads to talk skiing and powder (pure powder, you know?) over this, any day. Some of these people are over 40 years of age, they've raised children, or at least attempted to. Yet they take the time to sit down to publicly shame themselves and others through meaningless text in response to their peeves for the day (yes, well done, the irony of Kind Regards). Nonetheless, due to the average person being unwise and above all else nosey, the more personal people go with these ridiculous expressions of anger, the more attention these posts get and I've not even scratched the surface in here, yet. The harsher people go, the more likes, interactions and comments they get. Life has become a numbers game, particularly online. These people have online communities to support each other as well and there will be scenarios where more full-grown adults will pile in and begin arguing to tremendous length as to whether Hitler was vegan. It's incredible for all the wrong reasons. We're rubbish.

I just want cool videos of dogs and babies (call me broody, they're so cute).

People see celebrities (using that term loosely here) and want their life. Seeing people travel the world, meeting fans, enjoying their life has bred jealousy and anger for some of us not having the superstar lifestyle those we follow have. People aren't willing enough to do anything about it; they channel their emotions into abusing those who have a life they crave. It doesn't stop with celebrities and people of influence, however, it has become a constant competition to one-up people who are in our newsfeed. I've seen so many blanket statements beginning with 'Don't you hate it when', only to see that the remark is made to spite somebody else for something they have uploaded. Social media has turned the masses rather sour recently. We now have people succeeding for saying the most hateful things possible because they're seen as 'telling it like it really is'. One particular person quoting 'A final solution' when discussing British foreign borders (knowing full well the historical significance of what they'd cited), has been rewarded with newspaper columns and a radio show as well as countless TV appearances (though thankfully since initially typing this, the success of said person has slowly been halted). It's become a minefield, what was designed to bring us closer together has pushed us further apart. We have become even more selfish and ignorant.

Take Instagram for example. The app where we all upload the snippets of our life that mean the most to us: holidays, birthdays, celebrations, the extraordinary, sometimes the ordinary; it's the best of us. Online society has quickly learned that people are more interested in the 'what' and the 'where', before they become loyal to the 'who' in posting (unless you're trying to sleep with someone, in which case you'll continue to like any post from your mate-to-be until they reciprocate the action, then it's game on). Individuals now go to extreme lengths to improve their image online; to increase the attention they get. People will want to be seen 'living their best life' on social media (honestly that phrase needs burning at the stake), or constantly having fun, because nobody wants to see hard work or struggle, which would remind us of our own problems. That's how it works. There are apps to change the shape of our faces, whiten our teeth, tan our skin, make our eyes sparkle, remove spots and freckles, make us skinnier or make us more toned; it has become a circus. Why do we all subscribe to this lie? We're all aware of the apps, we know what our school friends look like before photo edits. We all like, comment and interact, but then also discuss with our friends that the photo does not depict an accurate representation of the person who posted. Does this not seem a little bit mental to anybody?

Our vanity has evolved out of the phone screen and into the real world. Many feel the need to put one foot directly in front of the other when posing for a picture as this makes their legs look slimmer apparently. All I see is someone looking like they're about to wet themselves. Some will tense their jawline to make their jaw squarer, to look like Henry Cavill, forgetting that they do not have the same jawline as Superman (handsome man). Another classic is the inner cheek bite to slim the face down and those who are real experts will be able to make it look like they have incredibly defined cheekbones. All I see is the face someone makes when they're sat on the toilet and they've just fallen victim to 'splashback' (splashback is the occurrence when the water in the toilet bowl splashes so hard, the water splashes upwards and makes contact with your skin; vile). The self-modifications are ridiculous. Nobody naturally stands with their hands holding the front of their hips while reaching around the front of the stomach, accompanied with high elbows to make hips look skinnier. Nor do topless people tense stomachs so hard that they look like they're midway through passing a kidney stone. We're all on board with this utter façade, showing our support through likes and pointless comments. Don't start me on the power of the emoji.

If we each stood along a scale rating from one to ten, I personally look at least one and a half better online than in real life. I am guilty of filtering to ensure my pasty, snow-white skin has some sort of tanned colour because it's the only time I have control of making myself look better. I have no idea why, maybe it's the fact I've been told I'm so pale I'm see-through. I was even once asked if I'd been on the moon beds. Credit where it's due, it was fairly funny, but I was only 17 and on a beach in Ayia Napa for my first holiday with friends (no parents, no vegetables, no bedtimes). I was pathetic enough being both the skinniest and palest person on Nikki beach; my confidence didn't need murdering like that. We all have our excuses.

A big issue for me is I have great difficulty posing for pictures. If I've got a drink in my hand it becomes easy, all I need to do is hold the drink at my midriff and allow my other arm to dangle loosely. I'd go as far as saying this is textbook when out. However, in the absence of a drink, what else is there to do? It's unnecessary stress figuring out what to do with my hands, do I throw my thumbs up as if to say to the camera, 'cool, man?'. Of course not, that would make me look weird. I can't let both arms hang loose either, if I do that, then I look stiff; it makes me look like I could commit a mass shooting at any moment. Would it be clenched fists or hands spread along the thighs? I have absolutely no chance of a career in modelling. Sometimes I just wish I had pigtails. There is no more confident poser than somebody with pigtails. They don't need a drink, or an accessory, all they need to do is tilt their head to one side grabbing a pigtail and that's it, easy, posing complete. My short back and sides (completely unadventurous trim) don't allow for this. I can't thread my finger through the kink in my hair that doesn't stretch more than two inches off my head. I'd just look like I had a receding hairline and I was trying to hold on. I also need to keep reminding myself that for every successful picture taken there are at least ten others to choose from.

Look out below

Social media has become more than a keyhole showing the best of our lives. The prophets of social media have begun alerting the world to the notion of normality; posting photos of themselves situated in rather extraordinary scenarios offering a reminder 'that you only see one per cent of a person's life on social media'. Inspirational. We've become more conscious to show the seemingly ordinary as much as possible. We don't like normal though. Friends will still discuss Instagram when planning a day out, or even a holiday. Social media dictates what we do, where we go and how we act. We increase our daily activity to show that no day seems the same. I've always wanted to skydive but have never committed to booking one. When I found out I could be filmed and share it online, I couldn't get on the plane quick enough (it was actually a birthday present from my girlfriend, who from now on will be referred to as 'EJ', given there's far more to her than the fact she's medically qualified; though she is so medically qualified). I arrived at Sibson Airfield in Peterborough, hungover from my birthday night out. Apparently, turning 24 is a pivotal moment in one's life, so warrants an overpriced burger and a night out with friends. Despite the hangover anxiety, I was optimistic that skydiving would be one of the best experiences I've had, ever. I think EJ was hoping for a chute malfunction and for me to fall to my certain death, what a birthday present that would be. We checked in and were told, of course, we were going to be in plane 12 of 14, so had to wait for two and a half hours on a bench with access to nothing but a tuck shop, watching 11 ecstatic groups head over to the small hangar in their overalls before shooting into the sky and make their way back down, though I could only see them once the parachutes had deployed. I managed to nap on the bench to nurse my hangover, though the early September heat, together with the garden bench, didn't set ideal conditions for a pre-jump snooze. After trying to sleep for what felt like an age, EJ shook me awake. Apparently we'd been called to the training centre (a Portakabin next door to the tuck shop). Our group packed in around one instructor who gave a 30-second discussion about dangling our legs out of the plane and keeping our body symmetrical during free fall. After this, we were fully qualified tandem skydivers (to my horror, you only need to take a six-hour class before being qualified to jump out solo; lunatics).

We hopped into our overalls before making our way to the launch pad where we awaited picking up. Despite being the twelfth group, I'd not taken the time to observe the plane taking me up. I heard a light buzz, like a lawnmower, humming away behind me. I turned around to see a vehicle no bigger than a fridge with a 20-foot wingspan, propellers and three steps hanging out from the door to climb aboard. I've never been less confident getting into a plane, but at least if it failed I'd be attached to a professional parachute artist.

Our videographer turned up just in time to document my disgust at the aircraft before ascending the stepladder to almost certain death. Led Zeppelin didn't mention the stairway to heaven was only three steps long; it's more underwhelming than the aircraft was. The plane had two benches parallel longways to each other, no seatbelts, no extra legroom option, certainly no business class section. I sat in the back right-hand corner of the plane, wedged between the legs of my tandem co-pilot whom I met there and then, while EJ sat calmly in the opposite corner (this wasn't her first rodeo).

The 13,000-foot climb seemed to take an eternity, I was camped in my own head with nowhere to go and every time I looked left there would be a camera in my face. The videographer was giving us our money's worth to be fair, but the camera was constantly six inches from my face and his favourite angle was catching all of my five chins. The journey wasn't helped by the classic zinger jokes from my tandem pilot about me not being clipped to him properly, because the only thing between being alive and falling to my death was the four clips attaching us. That's a lot of trust in a stranger. As the plane neared its summit, I peered out of the window to look down and immediately felt my stomach roll inside itself. My face drained and I looked away in the direction of another passenger, who laughed at me. She was about 60. I won't say I wanted her chute to fail, but I'd have laughed if she fell to her death. I was to be second-last out of the plane, with EJ last; as if this wasn't bad enough, I was going to have to watch the others go before me. The plane jolted suddenly, which apparently means the handbrake had been put on. I couldn't control my anus from quivering. We'd reached our summit, end of the line. It was time to make an orderly exit and jump back towards the Earth.

As the first passengers jumped, I realised how rapidly we'd be falling; they each disappeared from view in seconds. My stomach continued to turn and ached from the tension. I sat back watching in disbelief as one by one each person vanished. Just as I came to terms with what my eyes were showing me (to clarify, it was people jumping out of a plane), my pilot began to shuffle forward, pushing me towards the door. Oh my fuck. The insane cameraman had stepped out onto the side of the plane to film my exit from both the plane and life. The skydiver tapped me to help him shuffle to the door from the bench, which took every ounce of strength my jelly legs had. I didn't need to think about dangling my legs around the foot barrier as they were hanging from me like two pipe cleaners. I looked out at the curvature of the Earth (or the continuous flat bit depending on if you're wearing your tinfoil hat) and folded my hands to opposite shoulders as instructed. With a goofy smile on my face for the stupid cameraman (still getting my money's worth), I shook my head and begged, "No, please no."

But it was too late. We jumped.

After a disorientating two seconds of flipping, where my brain couldn't comprehend what was going on, I found myself staring at the Earth, feeling the full force of gravity pulling me. I was in flight, soaring through the air at blistering pace.

I was in free fall. No feeling in the world can replicate this, if you could bottle it, put it in a pill, or grind it up into a fine white powder with chalk, you'd be the wealthiest person alive. Nothing can compare to the feeling of complete free fall for 10,000 feet. I couldn't shout, I couldn't hear, I couldn't do anything but enjoy it. My entire body tingled with adrenaline firing through me. I was flying. I felt electric. I felt invincible. I felt the best feeling in the world as I watched the Earth get closer and closer, to the point where I thought, *this feels less than 3,000 feet. I've had my fun, pull it.* Then the fall came to a rather abrupt stop. My legs were flung upwards, as if I'd gone from belly down and rotated all the way to belly up from the force of the parachute deploying. Despite the several warnings from the instructor, I'll never remain as petrified as the split second where the harness dropped by an inch once the parachute successfully deployed. The inch of falling from your instructor feels like you're about to fall to your death, but before you come to terms with the fear, you're floating through the air, looking out at the magnificent world below. It was so beautiful.

I began to catch my breath and attempted to salivate, as my mouth was drier than the morning alarm situation. Sadly there was no room temperature water to pour down me. As I came to terms with the fact I'd just flown for almost a minute, all I could do was try and soak in the feeling, record every view and feeling in my body. It was even more electrifying than I'd expected. I felt an overwhelming calm as I looked out towards the land beneath me, a strange moment of relaxation despite the fact I was only four clips away from death, still.

"How was that for you, mate?"

I'd almost forgotten I was attached to another human being.

"Incredible, I can't believe it!"

I was shouting at the top of my lungs from the sheer

excitement and given the fact I was facing away from him, though we were tied to one another, proved awkward to converse. I continued to pant, in awe of how slow everything felt with the parachute now open. As life returned to a normal pace, I was able to think again, quickly realising I was in mid-air attached to someone else, and hanging in the air with us was this strange awkward silence that needed to be filled. My brain demanded I fill it. I felt compelled to talk to my tandem hero. There was no escape from the need for conversation. I didn't want to appear rude. Why should I enjoy gliding down to Earth in perfect silence? I had to say something.

"How many of these do you do a day then?"

That's the best I could do, the equivalent of a 'you been busy today mate?' I'd gone from flying through the atmosphere to sitting not only in a taxi, but on the driver's lap while he tells me this is just part of the job, but he still gets a buzz every time he does it. Right on, man. I pretended to be so interested in skydiving that I'd try and do a solo jump next (probably never going to happen). Needless to say, the two minutes that followed dulled the overall experience. I was too worried about making polite conversation with a stranger despite not even looking at his face, than enjoying the feeling of coming back down to Earth. He also thought it would be a good idea to show me how to get down quicker by turning the parachute sharply, which is like the spinning tea-cups ride in Disneyland on steroids. Safe to say I had no trouble salivating once we cranked through several turns. At least his tricks worked; it was soon time to land.

Skydive instructors are rather strict when it comes to landing; knees into your chest and feet up, their legs land first and you follow. Easy enough, right? We picked our spot around our man on the ground, who waved from below, still with his camera in hand. I hoisted my knees so they were practically touching my chin as we came in, though I felt like I could have defecated at any second when holding the position. The instructor was about to guide me home, safe and sound.

"Here we..."

That's all I heard. I was thrown forward, but my right leg got stuck underneath me. I'd no idea what had happened, but I was under a parachute and my leg was throbbing. It was so broken. My body instinctively lashed out to set me free,

"I'll unclip!" the instructor yelled.

He released me from the clips. I could barely put weight on my right foot; it hurt so much, but I was alive. I was on the ground and alive. I'd survived the jump, I'd survived the small talk, I'd survived a crash landing.

"How was that?"

The camera was back in my face. Fair play to this man, he was dedicated to his job, but now really wasn't the time. I had no idea what I said. According to the video I was sent I said, "I tell you what, I have no words for that."

I'm sceptical if it's real or voiced over and what I really said was, "He had one job."

Embarrassed by his woeful landing, the tandem instructor explained to me,

"We came in a bit quick," which he didn't seem to think I noticed.

Whether I had no words for the free fall or the crash landing I've no idea. As I knelt in the middle of an airfield, all I could think was how I was going to explain to my mother (whose only two requests of me are to never get a tattoo and never skydive or bungee jump) how I'd broken my leg doing a skydive.

I limped back to the base, arm in arm with EJ, who was obviously uninjured and completely relaxed; did she realise she'd just jumped out of a plane? EJ's calmness brought me down to earth a lot quicker than small talk and turning tricks with Captain Crash-landing; idiot.

As we got back to the garden bench centre, I did what any rebellious son does and called my parents to tell them how I'd skydived and survived. I anticipated a response of 'you're crazy you two!' You know the kind of response where your parents pretend to tell you off? Well, that's not what came.

"You [several expletives] idiot, how can you do this to me? I'll kill her an' all!"

My mum was not, I repeat, not happy. Not one bit. She hurled abuse down the phone at me (and some at EJ as well, which in truth was a welcomed change) and told me she didn't want to speak to me for a few days, nor did my dad. They buttoned the phone and refused to answer. Something about me risking my life though I'm probably more likely to die from being electrocuted while putting my phone on to charge than in a skydiving accident, though this information didn't help me at the time. I've no idea why I was so excited to tell my parents, but if truth be told, it ruined mine and EJ's mood that afternoon and always taints the memory of one of the most exhilarating minutes of my life (alongside losing my virginity, also tainted by how loud *Britain's Got Talent* was on the TV; it was like Ant and Dec were in the room congratulating me). We headed back to London with me in need of pizza and attention; the hospital could wait until the morning. I wasn't spending my Sunday evening in University College London Hospital. Sunday is my time (I didn't tell my parents about the broken leg; I thought best not).

After my X-ray the next morning it was surprising how quickly the doctor called me back in. Clearly, it was a simple diagnosis, they'd cast me up and send me home. I hobbled into the news of nothing broken, barely any bruising and politely being told I've got a lower pain threshold than an infant. Even better. No cool injury or scar to show from my dance with death, just my family not speaking to me for a week, a bad limp for a little longer and completely wasting the NHS time. I did get my favourite Instagram ever, with a really witty caption of 'Jumping to conclusions like...'

Don't worry I hate myself.

Peace sign and wink-face.

Put it down

I struggle to comprehend what adult life was like before phones (proper phones like iPhones and smartphones, not the Nokia brick). People must have done more than come home to watch terrestrial TV, or read a book or newspaper. My only memory is of my mum speaking on the landline for about an hour a day, either to her mum, dad, sisters, or maybe a friend now and again. What's changed? It doesn't take long once I'm back in my flat to be bored. I only cook once or twice a week as EJ enjoys it as part of her evening. I'm also banned from cooking after any alcohol consumption (after a nasty episode involving fish). While cooking we play music, so I can't watch the TV, hence I quickly turn to burying my head in my phone while conversing in autopilot mode. The only barometer I have to check how I'm doing is social media. Though I shouldn't, I can compare if the people around me are feeling the same or having the same experiences in adult life. Is this where my addiction comes from, the feeling that we're all in it together?

We try our utmost to impress our followers online, desperate to match or even trump the lives they lead, so they too believe the illusion that our everyday life is fantasy. The daily grind has become daily Donald as we now live trying to one-up each other. We're more concerned about making an impression. The worst of the daily Donalders are the people who continually post about loving their job (of course I am unable to love mine, therefore I'm jealous). Though I could deceive people into thinking my job is amazing if I was invested in my social media profile enough, but I refuse to live such a lie. Perhaps I am just miserable and unwilling to accept the position I'm in. The only time I will broadcast my working life to the world is if I'm in the office past midnight (which has only happened about 20 times in fairness), voicing my opinion that I am underpaid and too disinterested to be doing so. It's the routine eight to nine finishes that make me miserable. I wish I had a good work ethic, like those people who can pull 15-hour days and get on with it. Usually, they're working in an investment bank so earn double my salary in their Christmas bonus alone; I still don't think it's enough of an incentive. I appreciate that any person should be allowed to enjoy their life however it may be, we all have our obstacles to overcome, but I cannot get on board with the continual posting and promotion of (most likely false) enjoyment of a job. I do not care for views from offices around the UK, or how a hotel room in southern England looks when the company expenses pay for it. I struggle to understand the urge to post and promote every move we make; vloggers must be insane. I couldn't choose to unfollow people because I'd be out of the loop. I'd miss out. I'm far too curious (nosey) for that. I can't help my continuous disgust at the 'how's your Monday' attitude pandemic, coming from holidaymakers who take five Mondays off each year, excluding bank holidays, but feel the need to alert the world. It is weekend millionaire mentality. It is jealousy on my part; jealous I'm not careless enough to be like them. Despite my hatred of the extraordinary being bragged about as false normality, social media is ultimately at its worst when people decide to document and post the absolute ordinary.

Careful what we wish for.

At least if social media is filled with travelling or people living their best lives, our minds wander and we long for something unexpected ourselves. However, when somebody makes the conscious decision to share pictures of their new furniture, having their nails done, or a meal they've cooked from home, it just becomes depressing. Do you feel the need to share this part of your life, really? Isn't this what WhatsApp and close friends are for? Home-cooked meals are usually dreadful to look at as well. They should come with a warning. I understand that effort has gone into any meal, even beans on toast (never cheese, by the way). There is genuine effort when cooking, from the purchasing of the posh garlic bread as a side dish, to the garnish on top of a risotto, but what is the point in uploading it online? We want to see food cooked by Gordon Ramsey, Jean Imbert, even Jamie Oliver (despite him apparently being responsible for the removal of chocolate from the vending machines in my school), not amateur Annie's soggy spaghetti bolognese in Balham with cheap garlic bread eaten off the chopping board. At least buy the posh one. People now need credit for any small effort they make; cooking a meal has now become an achievement despite eating being one of the most natural events we experience, on par with excretion. I should note there is a genuine Twitter page where people rate each other's poo. Humans are so grim. Social media is meant to entertain us. If we are bored (usually by those most active) of that which was designed to cure our boredom, then we are simply wasting time, sitting around, staring vacantly into a screen six inches from our face and waiting to die. That isn't all.

This innovation has led to an invasion. Online advertising is forced upon us as the supposedly small price we pay for using these platforms. Often these are targeted towards the account holder, so mine personally are filled with a strange mixture of film adverts, sports book betting offers (the irony of them saying 'when the fun [of gambling] stops, stop'), new restaurants and gifts related to the presents I purchased for

Secret Santa up to three years ago. Some algorithm believes I am a Donald Trump ultra-fan because I bought a wonderful American colleague a 'Make America Great Again' cap two years ago. Wit at its finest. I still receive emails asking if I'm interested in books about Trumpisms or other Donald-related merchandise. I'll pass. I'm still unsure how I'm meant to answer the question, "Did you enjoy your 'Make America Great Again' cap?" Do people enjoy caps? I am helpless, like everyone else, as I have no option to turn away from this harassment. I cannot envisage walking out of a shop having bought a pair of trainers, for other shop clerks to run after me waving other trainers similar to the pair I've just purchased, shouting, 'It's because you liked those trainers!' That would defeat the purpose of the entire trip. But every company has to make their money somehow. It's painful when all I want to do is sit quietly alone and mindlessly kill time by peeking into other people's lives, but every five seconds I am directed to a website I clicked on six months ago. I'm sure I saw something about 'mature over-forties near [me]' on my dad's computer once. Never mind. The burden of advertising is even more annoying when EJ uses my laptop to look at household accessories, clothes, or medical apparatus, which leads to my phone being continuously spammed for furniture, bikinis and Botox numbing cream. All I want to see is a good holiday destination, what a film set looks like, or how athletes train at a professional level. Is that really too much to ask?

Through the social media movement, our obsession with phones has led to us living our lives with a lens pointing at everything we see. Our experiences are now obstructed by other people's desire to use their phones to capture the best angle. Festivals and concerts are supposed to be experiences when we're lost in a moment with an artist and the surrounding crowd. From purchasing a ticket to being stood in the midst of thousands, the anticipation we feel to see an idol, an inspiration, or just the music that makes us happy (or just makes us feel, if you're super edgy) kills us, as we wait for the arrival on stage of the act we're desperate to see. We've all shrieked with excitement when the lights go out for the show to begin. Only now it's tougher to see these idols in the flesh. We must endure the opening minutes battling to see past the thousands of phone screens that steal our view. Some will go to see an artist to let others know that they are present at the gig everybody wants to be at, without having much of an interest. They'll stand there, loosely wave their phones above their head to create a video they will almost certainly never watch again, but their followers will know they were there. I was at a gig in Finsbury Park during the best summer ever (summer of 2018), where I experienced this behaviour at its worst.

I was lucky to grow up with friends who showed me different music genres and artists in school, so by the time I got to university I had already discovered historic artists like Oasis, The Beatles or Queen, which in turn didn't force me to buy a bucket hat, smoke rolled up cigarettes and drink nothing but mixed berry Dark Fruits for three years. Right on, brothers and sisters (meanwhile I picked up a strange obsession for Kanye West and Jay-Z, which had no influence on the way I dressed; I know what I can't pull off). Being 13 when Oasis split up, my friends and I didn't have the chance to see a band we grew up loving (except for a lucky few), therefore I saw the chance to see Liam Gallagher in concert as my Oasis, and in Finsbury Park in the height of summer; what a night it would be. Finally, I'd get to hear their lyrics from the main man and not a parody group at Mathew Street Music Festival in Liverpool (not quite the same). We got to the park in plenty of time for a few drinks and to get into a sound space with enough room that I wouldn't be squashed when everybody started bouncing, or lose a shoe as I did at a gig aged 14. I wish I could pretend it was for a cool band, but no, it was at a Fall Out Boy concert. I was 14. (I did reclaim the shoe before the concert ended). We secured our space and spread out, giving ourselves a bit of elbow room to hold our drinks about half an hour before Liam Gallagher (or if you're a cool person, LG) would take to the stage and send us supersonic.

A group of girls/young women (call them what you want, they were a similar age to me, maybe slightly younger) about ten strong, wearing classic dance festival attire (we'll get to that) waltzed in front of us about five minutes before the start; typical. Though I saw them as encroaching on our space and it being an insult to our good time planning, it was a public park. I could do nothing and the excitement was too much to worry about them and their wellies (most of them had wellies on despite being in a London-based park in the middle of summer). As the sun was setting to the right-hand side of the stage, the music humming through the speakers stopped and the lights went out; it was time. The band members took to the stage and gave their instruments one final check; the crowd roared. I felt pathetic at how excited I was, struggling to contain my grin at the empty stage in front. But the view of the stage was rather short-lived, as each of the group in front (along with thousands of others) began waving their phones above their heads at my eye level, just as the band began playing 'Rock 'N' Roll Star'. I had to stretch my chin to the sky to keep the front of the stage in sight above the thousands of outstretched hands clutching phones. Once Liam Gallagher flew out and the crowd started bouncing, I had to accept my fate; I could only see him if I concentrated hard enough. To make matters worse, we were in some sort of sound black spot, so the music sounded like it was coming out of a car radio (which I'd know all about because my mates and I would steal it after the show and take it back to

Liverpool with all the other stolen car stereos because we're from Liverpool and we steal things).

My group jumped around clinging to one another, screaming out, "Tonight, I'm a rock 'n' roll star!"

No ability to sing between us, just holding each other and jumping up and down with the hope no warm pints hit us. This shouldn't be confused with an attempt to dance by the way. It's just a bit of an excited pogo; definitely no lip biting. What a night this was going to be, even if we were louder than the music ourselves. As the crowd calmed following the first chorus, we regrouped, counted how many drinks we had left between us, as nearly all of them had been spilled, and got ready for the second wave. The sea of phones remained above the crowd, meaning the front of the stage was still difficult to see if you weren't at least six feet six inches tall.

We then noticed one of the group in front had clearly taken too much (probably) ketamine. The giveaway to this was how impressively bendy her arm and entire body were. She uncontrollably waved her phone about three inches from my face as she slurred the words, "She's Electric."

I should have pulled the bucket hat down over her eyes and sat her down; she probably wouldn't have known the difference – She's Electric – I'm not sure if it was a request or she was just having her own concert. Fair play to her for being able to speak at all; she looked like an inflatable tube person they have outside of car washes in America, absolutely all over the show. This set the tone for the entire evening – watching a concert being live-streamed through hundreds of phones despite actually being present. Win some, lose some. Unfortunately for my friends, the She's Electric mishap didn't compare to one of our own, who turned to me about 45 minutes into the set and asked, "When's Liam Gallagher coming on?"

This was his first and last experience with MDMA.

Great night.

You out tonight?

Social media has made us all desperate to make our lives look as fun as possible. We want to look both sociable and interesting to our followers despite not having any meaningful relationship with the vast majority of them. Still, every drink we have, meals we eat, everyday excursions and nights out are broadcasted to our followers. Days and nights out have gone from getting drunk with mates and having a laugh to continuous posing for the evening's stories and the next day's upload. There's a complete rigmarole to a night out now. I can only try to put myself in the shoes of a social media legend (hereon, referred to as SML) seeing as I seem to follow enough.

Beginning with the fresh trims, make-up artistry by our girlies, outfit changes (a good three or four), serial posters will want everybody to know their full intention of going out to drink and do the dancing. Those travelling home or to a different city will let people know from the moment they're in transit. Usually, a photo of their train ticket in hand and designer cardholder in the background so followers know they're in for a white-knuckle ride. Watch this space. The first post by an SML is a feeler post. People who create such content pretend they're broadcasting their whereabouts to their lucky followers; but we all know it's not for the many, it's for the special few (kind of the polar opposite to recent British Labour party manifestos). The early post is to throw bait to the several people the SMLs want to see it. Bait is laid with the blind hope someone they've been flirting for months with, by exchanging likes, bumps into them. It's 21st-century courting. After the feeler has gone out, there comes a period of radio silence while the physical preparation commences and the evening gets underway. The first shot uploaded is the first drink – lager, prosecco, wine – nothing too fancy; nobody peaks too early. It's just letting fans and friends know the drinking has commenced and they're underway. So exciting.

It's rare to find a pre-drink venue where there's an absence of phones. It's the prime time for pictures following the slog of getting ready and it's the main reason anybody goes to the efforts they do for going out to the same bars every week. Pictures being taken all over, flashes going off like the middle of a lightning storm; it's crucial to capture every angle and every moment for the next day's 'Best night with the best people [insert two or three emojis]' post. There's always one member of the squad late because they're shaving their pubes, waxing their legs, or curling their eyelashes, so the pictures continue until everybody is present and photographed. There's a classic pyramid structure of pre-drink photos for each group. For example, in each group of five, there will be a photo for every combination of five, four, three, two, and of course, the individual snaps. One foot in front of the other, cheeks sucked in, jaw tensed, shoulders back, and arms strategically placed; we know the score. After the groundbreaking insight of someone else getting ready, we watch pre-drinks unfold and decode some inside jokes being captioned on the Instagram stories that make no sense to anybody but those in the pictures. Still, we continue to watch. Before we know it, we're seeing smudged make-up, spilled drink marks, lipstick everywhere (male and female) and sweaty foreheads glistening in the light of a camera flash. It's absolute carnage and I wish I was present at every single one I've seen. I would wish to be if it wasn't for the fact I can smell the bad breath through my screen from the state people are in at this point. If only we could all have a night out as good as the people we follow. It's all fun and games until the trademark white girl video comes out (note the trademark white girl can be performed by anybody). This involves a video from above, tilting the phone downwards like a spotlight and swinging your head side-to-side, pretending to be a mermaid, a unicorn, or something else fab. In the same way, there's also the white guy (same rules apply), which involves classic nodding of the head, cheeky smile at the camera, and belting out the words with your mouth a little too close to your phone, so all we can hear is a slurred, shouted rendition to the big night out's soundtrack. Biting of own lips will often make an appearance.

After the dust has settled the following morning and the kebab meat on their bedside tables has hardened overnight, we see the final piece to this meddling puzzle. The declaration that the night was indeed a funny one, a fab one, or even the best one, in the form of a final post the next morning containing a group shot for us all to see. Heartwarming, but this is why I don't watch Instagram stories anymore. My life gains nothing from watching people (whom I don't know) enjoying themselves. I'm not interested in seeing what people do every weekend. I only ask in work through politeness, so I've given up on the world of SMLs because they offer nothing to me. Nights out are much more fun with real stories to be told, not just the same bar every week for five years. By real stories, I mean something like narrowly escaping being murdered with two dear friends after an impromptu Thursday evening out at karaoke. Real memories with real people.

To make it crystal clear, 'real memories with real people' was ironic. Can you imagine? (I just needed an excuse to tell this story.)

Being an August baby I was a year behind the field, so had started going out routinely in Liverpool by the age of 16, while in my sixth year of school. Going out before the age of

18 was much more exciting, but hectic. The constant scramble in the week leading up to going out involved begging older brothers and sisters for their passports, or for their friends' driving licences. We'd have to remember and regurgitate new names, birthdays, addresses. We'd even find out our new star sign to combat the doorman ingeniously asking what our star sign was. Nobody wants to be caught out on star signs. Being so young, I used to look forward to going out then having friends stay at my house so we could play on the Xbox the next morning; what a life. Still new to town, we'd go to bars that served flavoured shots and shooters because we thought it was cool to listen to dance music and drink blue Hercules tequila shots until we threw up (which didn't take long. Nights out at this age cost me no more than £40 as going for food afterwards didn't seem to be a thing back then either). After spending a few hours in these places, we'd end up being in a state, and taxis home would involve dizzy heads desperate to make the journey without being sick.

In October 2010 this was no different. We'd done plenty of pointing at each other, screaming song lyrics and bouncing around, until the £40 I had turned into £5 and it was time to head home with my two usual taxi shares. Only this time, one member of the party was unable to last the 12-minute journey to my house and quietly began throwing up in the rear of the seven-seater vehicle taking us home. Credit where it's due I didn't hear him. I only suspected something when the other brother put his hand on my shoulder and said, "Down the bottom and turn right," just as I was about to tell the driver to pull up as we were at my house.

Only then did I turn round and smell the tomato pasta vomit, which had been hurled into the footwell behind me (I was in the middle row of the car alone, no idea why). We turned the corner and pulled up, we now knew we'd be getting out and walking in the opposite direction of the taxi.

We eased out slowly, thanked, paid with a generous tip of £1 and, began power walking back to my house where we could claim sanctuary. About 15 seconds after our marching commenced, the horn beeped (despite it being past four in the morning in a residential area) and the formerly polite driver yelled, "You horrible twats" out of his window and began revving into a three-point turn.

Oh hell. The beep of his horn was our cue and we bolted to the bottom of the road, planning how we'd get away from the crazy man in the people van. We turned the corner and were in the clear heading towards my parents' house, but I knew with our only access being via slow-moving electric gates ('twat' seems accurate now I think about it), we wouldn't have time to open and close them without the driver seeing, thus catching and almost certainly murdering us. We had to hide.

The family-friendly engine roared as he shot towards the bottom of the road after us. He braked so hard at the turning, the tyres screeched. I dread to think where the vomit was going in the turbulent ride, probably would've made it worse but I can't imagine he was the type of man to take such information on board easily. It was a real manhunt. We soon found a hiding place at the bottom of the longest drive on the road. It was a narrow, 100 yard stretch of blackness, so dark that it consumed anything near it; the perfect hiding place. We sprinted down and hid among an ivy bush hanging on the right-hand wall. The ivy rustled around us as the winter breeze whistled through the night, causing us to shiver. It was still better than getting caught by this lunatic. The engine fell silent.

"You twats," he continued to yell, with no regard for the residents in their slumber.

It felt like a case of a pot meeting a kettle, but I wasn't going to give away our position. All we could do was wait in silence, but being stood clutching an enormous bush with your two oldest friends causes a couple of nervous giggles. Much like in school when a teacher tells you not to laugh as you sit there with a smirk on your face desperate to burst; we had to battle. Despite not being able to see each other, we could hear the sniggering and heavy breathing, trying not to laugh. I tried to shush the others, but this was interrupted by my own laugh, which in turn set one of the others off.

"Rats!"

Our attention turned to the top of the road again, where the car was inching past the elongated driveway. I covered my face to cease any noise coming from me, knowing any slight giveaway meant it was all over.

As the family wagon rolled past the gateway, the engine picked up and began rustling down the road. We waited for ten seconds then a phone screen lit up to give us the all-clear. We would get away with it this time. The taxi drivers' union may be up in arms at that story, I would be too knowing someone involved in my profession was mugged off by three teenagers; great fun nonetheless. Sadly none of the above was documented for social media mainly due to technological advancements of the time (think I had a Blackberry with the little rolling ball as a cursor; what a throwback). If I'd have even attempted to record the events that evening I'd be long gone, found dead in a skip miles away on the outskirts of Liverpool, covered in my friend's mum's regurgitated tomato pasta.

Mamma mia.

Modern behaviour

Everything must be shared. We're convinced that we're all unique forgetting that we share the same experiences. People will go on holiday to places they've seen based on Instagram, only to find out the holiday isn't worth the expense for one picture and a few likes. Many engaging in social media will share their interests and hobbies in an attempt to show what makes them different, which is positive, I believe; well, it depends really. Being acquainted with zoologists, unfortunately, exposes me to the horrors of insects and arachnids on my newsfeed. I've no idea how one can share a picture of a particular insect nurturing its offspring and branding it 'too cute' with several love hearts slapped underneath. Tech companies ought to be more responsible in ensuring such displays of distressing content don't surface on their sites; it's out of control.

Our obsession with smartphones has turned us from the social butterflies we supposedly once were into distrustful beings who keep our friendship circles tight and rarely go out to meet new people unless mutually swiping right and fancy some casual sex (sadly this never happened for me). If we ever find ourselves on a night out talking to a stranger, we have no trust. If we're asked to share our phone numbers to keep in touch, it's far safer to give a false one and not have to worry about stranger danger. It's just a phone number, why would we be so distrustful of a person standing in front of us? We give out our name, number, home address, email address, mother's maiden name, grandmother's birth certificate, first pet, the first road we lived on, and much more to anonymous companies solely in exchange for a two-minute clickbait article. I'll be hooked in with something like, 'You'll never guess what Wayne Rooney said about his former teammate…' – only to find the article says that he apparently thought Cristiano Ronaldo was the best player he played with. Riveting stuff. We've become so trusting of the internet, yet so backward when speaking to people. Why is it we feel under much more pressure when a person asks for our number instead of a company? When asked, we feel like we have to make a swift judgement call. Unlike clickbait, we'll only give out our number to people if there is something meaningful we seek; but it doesn't tend to happen on the first date. We must first be courted by follows and friend requests. They're so much different, aren't they?

In situations that require the swift judgement call of whether to give my number to someone, I (of course) panic and decide to provide false contact details. But I've no idea how to invent an entirely new phone number on the spot. I have to gamble on reciting the first ten numbers of the 11 number sequence, of my phone number, and change the final digit, from zero to eight. How can I be so uninventive? My number has been the same for 12 years. It's almost as if my brain wants me to be kind to the man who barely introduced himself at a bar in Soho before diving straight into telling me he'd recently divorced after a 16-year marriage. Now he was alone in a nightclub buying me tequila and asking for my number. Just as I arrived at the final digit, my mind pulled out changing the zero to an eight; maybe like he should've done with his ex-wife by the sound of her. He told me she was keeping the kids.

We've become so sceptical of the world around us. Granted everybody has their reasons to have doubts in an entity of some sort: corporate, government, charity, religion. People are losing faith in the bodies that once brought us together. Even friendships are now tested through social media; my own friends are unable to go out without me and me not finding out that evening; it's unfair on them. Of course, I wasn't bitter, nor was I then forced to become distrustful of those friends of mine. It was social media's fault, not theirs. The only positive was that I was spared from a night out in Clapham.

It seems we spend much more time with our extended circles because of social media and as a result, the relationships we have are tested more frequently. We can have deep discussions with our friends at any waking moment but are also able to be far nastier than in person. Arguments occur over WhatsApp because it is far easier to type aggressively to a friend or foe than it is to argue face-to-face. This is usually why people hide behind passive-aggressive emails and sign them off with 'Kind regards'. More arguments occur between WhatsApp groups because they are active for 17 hours a day. Talking behind people's backs has now become much easier to do. We no longer have to wait to meet a friend to start talking about someone else behind their back: we can simply open up a new chat, even a new group chat and moan privately. Though this does increase our levels of paranoia and before any message is sent I'll take a few seconds to triple check the group I'm posting to is the correct one and doesn't include the person I'm talking about. We've evolved from two-faced to poly-faced (poly-faced sounds better than multi-faced).

It's toxic.

Social media now influences our habits, where we go, what we do, it even holds influence over the places we eat. It's the ultimate marketing tool because we allow it to be. We upload pictures of coffee cups displaying our names with abysmal spelling, or we upload the flower walls of the restaurant we're sat in and it's all for marketing. It's like we've fallen into the biggest trap without knowing it, except for the conspiracy theorists. I've lost count of how many gimmick venues look fantastic through a lens but can barely put together a croque-monsieur (or if you're not fluent in French, a ham and cheese toasty) and we continuously fall for them. The latest craze is themed bars, which have taken off to infinite likes and beyond, despite being utter letdowns (sadly no *Toy Story* themes anywhere except Disneyland). Much like the *Peaky Blinders* themed bar in Liverpool (where much of the show was filmed, despite the rest of UK Twitter being up in arms because it is set in a different part of the country), which disappoints because people aren't able to pull off flat caps like Cillian Murphy after drinking there. I didn't go there, but I was left equally disappointed by a bar in London that sells cocktails based on children's novels. On arrival, I found out that the dream catcher jar (based on the *Big Friendly Giant*) only lights up because of a plastic ice cube with a light in it, and the cocktail tastes like bubble gum vodka, which is garbage. We've all fallen into the trap.

We put our lives out to our followers and they make a judgement based on what we show them; though I'm not sure we'd enjoy hearing everybody's thoughts. We've forgotten social media was meant for fun and we've allowed these caricature versions of ourselves to dictate who we are. We deserve all the judgement we get.

Chapter VI – Who are you to judge?

Judgement

We're quick to judge. Definitely too quick. It's natural and something we cannot control. Our minds are programmed to assess situations for danger, which is reflected in society when we judge whether we can trust those in front of us. We can be rational with our judgement, just as we can be irrational. I'll use an example from when I was on the tube (we're back) and two young men, probably in their twenties, were sat down near me, quietly laughing together. Two people on a Friday night enjoying a conversation in my favourite place, probably theirs too (I love the tube so much). I was stood with my brother, also enjoying a conversation about what Christmas presents we were sorting for our family Secret Santa (family Secret Santa goes down a storm every year, it's a big deal). Unfortunately, another person made a judgement in his head, which he struggled to act rationally on and so pointed to the two young men sat opposite him and screamed, "You are gay!"

He really yelled, as if he was witnessing a crime and snitching. My brother and I jumped from the shock of how loud he was, despite us being stood at the far end of the carriage. When I heard his voice I thought he was about to kill us all. My heart pounded, as we're reminded every day that any sudden movement or noise is probably a terrorist. I've never heard such loud screams in an enclosed space; the lunatic. He couldn't stop at "You are gay," he had to carry on with one final observation.

"Not straight!"

At least he was clear about what he meant. I think every witness to the incident found solace in the clarification that his unprompted accusation of two young men being gay did, in fact, mean they were not heterosexual. Good exam technique at least. The entire carriage was stunned with silence. My brother wanted to go and ask the man if he was okay and where his problem lay but in slightly more colourful language. I told him to hang back as there were young children sat next to the man who looked in distress already, though I felt in the wrong for not letting him do so. Thankfully, after screaming his witty quip, he buried his head into his bag and pretended to reorganise its contents, before heading to the door as the train pulled in.

In this case, there were no public displays of affection to each other from the two young men. I've seen plenty of necking on the tube and it knocks me sick. I've no idea how you'd be able to tell if they were together as friends, brothers, or in a relationship. People refuse to believe my brother and I are related as he looks like an actual supermodel and I look like, well, me. Yet this man felt the need to point out the judgement he had given them. It's difficult to understand why someone would roar at two people for having a laugh. Some of us just behave more rationally. Though hardly anything happened – in the grand scheme it was just an insignificant tube ride with my brother – this story sticks with me because it showed me how inconsiderate and ignorant people can be. Do I change the world and make good of all evil or do I stay in my lane, making sure I'm kind to others? Will prioritising my own behaviour make me selfish?

I'd be an awful superhero.

I've always tried to be courteous to those around me, going out of my way to be kind, for I've no idea what's going on in somebody else's life. But does it pay to be kind all the time? We now come to the defining rave, my eureka moment, which, through my own passing of judgement (though I am rational and keep it to myself or wait until a later time to tell people in private as I should), I changed my behaviour. I changed my way of thinking forever. This was the day everything changed. I've no idea why.

Raving, but not misbehaving

I'm not massively into house music. I struggle to listen to it alone (unless it's created by my dear friend, Acer), but if I'm to socialise with my friends in London, being all cool because they live in London, it's a medium I must endure. There's a huge movement that involves listening to this music; designed to, when accompanied with a series of bright lights, lasers, and possibly chemical experimentation, make us relax and feel in ways we couldn't otherwise experience in everyday life. On occasion, I've flirted with this scene, mainly to spend more time with my friends in London. They'd leave me behind otherwise and I don't want that, I'm with my thoughts enough as it is. I'd never want to feel alienated from the people I call friends.

I'm unsure if it was me growing up and becoming more aware of it, or if I was involved in some sort of epidemic, but about the age of 19, I started to notice how so many people use drugs on nights out. Once I noticed it for the first time I couldn't ignore it. Every toilet trip I was serenaded by a chorus of snorting, in urinals or cubicles, even people stood at the bar. Weren't they meant to be super-illegal?

It's now part of the status quo. Whether they've become too easy to get hold of, or our generation needs them to escape from reality (which is rubbish), I've no idea. Every night out, jaws are swinging, lips are sucked and pupils are like black holes coming to eat your soul. It's easy to see who is and isn't getting on it. For a start, people taking cocaine on a night out feel the need to gaze around the room with their widened eyes, scanning the floor like owls as they prepare to pass the bag from one to another. At least these folk try to mask what they're doing, which is probably why it's so obvious because they all look like they're somewhere between surprised, disgusted, and angry. However, it's a slightly different ball game at an organised commercial rave, where my attitude towards life changed forever.

Before upgrading to super-cool London-standard raves, I'd been to a few during my time at university, for no other reason than curiosity. I was curious to see how powder and pills could make a room of people dance to music in such a loving way, as my housemates had told me. They'd wake up from their raves (admittedly as shells of themselves) and tell me of the magical night they'd had, how they could feel the music and got lost in the lights. It was a pretty great advert for something I'd been told never to entertain the idea of for 20 years. But what are we without our curiosity? We must not hide from questions we want the answers to and as my friendship circle became more experimental, the question grew inside; how good can they be?

Eventually, I tagged along, but instead of feeling like a young, experimental liberal, living life on a knife-edge with my peers, I was more of an out-of-place, trying to get down with the kids, fool. I could not help but pass judgement at these events as I quickly noticed that, for some, it was more of a competition about who could be edgier. Wavy garments weren't something I was prepared for (wavy garments are when ravers use the event as an excuse for dressing like a total dickhead). Hawaiian shirts, bucket hats, jeans rolled up to mid-calf, showing at least three inches of white trainer socks and some Reebok classic trainers that have been

Chapter VI – Who are you to judge?

covered in mud for dramatic effect. Cool man. These are the same people who were doing horse riding and calling their parents 'Mummy' and 'Daddy' until they were 17. No, I didn't do horse riding.

I attended my first rave in the University of Sheffield's student union in my final year; wearing a Jurassic Park pyjama top, for no other reason than it was the comfiest I owned at the time because I was so paranoid about being as relaxed as possible. It didn't really look like a pyjama top either; I got away with wearing it out. I think I may have been using it to sleep in at the time (it's acceptable to wear t-shirts to sleep in between October and February). It didn't help me relax, ravers were approaching me from the get-go and the t-shirt was getting all the plaudits. I couldn't quite believe it. Wearing my pyjama top for the fact that I was scared gave me exactly what I didn't want, attention. One of the rare occasions I haven't welcomed it. Would people pass the same judgement on to me? Did they think I was playing their game of dressing like I'd found my clothes in an overturned eBay lorry? There's nothing worse than the feeling that you are part of something you claim to laugh at and don't want to be a part of. This was my first and last science fiction t-shirt I'd wear at raves. From then on it was plain t-shirts and hoodies, just to show people that I'm not one of them. I can't wait to walk around permanently dressed like a dad at a barbecue; a pale blue shirt shrouded by the ultimate dad accessory, the half zip. When I find myself dressed in this, wearing a sensible pair of slacks, I'll know I'm where I want to be. Sadly, for raves it must be a hoody, to tie around my waist for when I'm in full two-stepping motion and getting a sweat on. The art of two-stepping for me is more plodding than anything else, lifting one foot about half an inch off the floor and back down, and then repeating with the other. Minimal movement, I'm a terrible dancer remember.

149

The defining rave

This London rave was a defining day in my life. It would be one to remember from the moment I set foot into my taxi to the abandoned warehouse. I had the usual crippling anxiety, asking myself, *What if my parents were to see me?* I sat there, pondering how badly they'd disprove; it begs the question, *Why did you go?* Until this day I'd go to extreme lengths to keep up socialising with my friends. It is on these occasions, events such as bank holiday weekend raves, that I get to spend time with them; it's either that or binge through a couple of adventure films in my pyjamas for the umpteenth time, dreaming of another world. In truth, without those events, aside from playing football (we say football doesn't count) I'd miss out on some of our best nights together. I live north of the river, 40-plus minutes away on the tube, it is a lot of effort to casually see each other and they rarely venture up to my end. How could I not attend these events? I'd go mad if all I did was watch films and fantasise about a life with more meaning than mine, inspired by science fiction and mythology. Also, I'm a massive 'yes' man (boy).

Before I'd even arrived, I knew I didn't want to be there. To think, if my mum or dad saw me now, what would they say? I dread the thought so much. I'd use my curiosity to battle the guilt, which I've only done a handful of times in my entire life. This was just like being back in university. I was in my taxi, sweating, as usual, attempting to reassure myself that I am a good person. I went through the ritual of telling myself I don't steal, nor do I cause harm, I don't manipulate anybody, I'm polite. This is just a chemical experiment at the age of 23, nothing more. The worry built up to the natural level of me feeling sick in my stomach, to the point where I needed to either throw up or have a nervous poo; a great start.

I'm unsure why, but when the slightest feeling comes where

I need to sit on a toilet, there is no turning back. It's high alert, code brown. *Oh no*, I thought, knowing I had to find somewhere immediately. The code brown made me sweat more than I was used to. I tried to place my mind elsewhere, thinking about how I was going to have a great day with my friends, getting to spend some quality time together on another planet. Hang on, were we? Or were we just going to two-plod next to each other for eight hours and barely utter three words to each other. Cool. My stomach began to cramp as the cogs turned inside. The taxi pulled up to the venue and the thought of my parents was a distant memory. I shot out of the taxi and dashed through the car park to the abandoned warehouse, preparing to make a dirty protest to no one but my trousers. I knew it was bad as I contemplated going in a drugs amnesty wheelie bin that I passed on my way in.

Fortunately, the queue was a short one, as was the drugs search; hardly a thorough exercise in one in these venues. It's more just a patting down as a box-ticking exercise. They'd never check my boxer shorts, though if I didn't find a toilet in the next two minutes they wouldn't need to. The warehouse was enormous, perhaps it was an old distribution centre, with three open-plan floors, two courtyards bigger than football pitches, and the main toilets on the far side, just past Mordor. I struggled to run as I felt my hips relax in preparation for delivering the poo-baby I was about to give birth to. As I weaved my way through the labyrinth, I turned the corner to the main toilets and – no. The queue to the three cubicles was at least 50 hipsters long, each blitzed out of their brains already. I didn't have time to analyse their dress, I had to find another place to defecate or it would be an early taxi home for me. I was about to run out of time and lose all dignity until I thought of one way to lose just a little of my dignity. I rushed to the nearest steward.

"Excuse me, mate, I have Crohn's disease and I'm about

to-"

"Follow me!"

After cutting me off, the steward turned and sprinted to a wooden panelled door guarded by a security team of two. Please.

I followed (which annoyed me because I see myself as more of a shepherd than a sheep, but there was no time to be too contentious with my own principles), clutching my stomach in desperation. The two enormous men parted to allow us through and we darted through a series of double doors down a stretched, eerie corridor, until he halted about 200 yards away from where we'd entered. It was only here I realised I'd blindly followed a stranger down a dark corridor for no other reason than he was wearing a pink high visibility bib and an earpiece; still, needs must. He pointed to a thin wooden door that was barely six feet tall, stuck on the front was a laminated sheet of paper displaying the letters 'VIP'.

I ran through it being so desperate and I leapt for the toilet to relieve myself. I could finally take a second to calm myself thanks to this very important poo. Everything was going to be okay. After a brief sit, taking time to tell myself I would enjoy the next few hours, I jumped up, rinsed my hands and face with freezing water, and headed back through the haunted corridor towards the bar for a well-earned beer. At the bar, I rubbed shoulders with the usual bucket-hat hipsters and I battled my way for a drink before meeting my chums. I figured that once I met them, I may as well tell them about the horrendous journey from my front door to the Earth's core to relieve myself, because after that initial conversation, they'd struggle to remember anything else I told them, other than maybe if I said I love them, which always seems to go down well.

I slipped away from the bar, two tins of beer (the worst kind by the way) in hand, and turned the corner to head for the dance floor. The music evolved from a distant beat to an overpowering thud that was vibrating through every bone in my body. I could feel the weight of the bass in my chest as I struggled to adapt and catch my breath. The visuals were equally breathtaking; lights and lasers shot through the air in patterns that wowed my mind. I was fascinated more than excited, but knew with my friends I'd enjoy myself. They caught my eye waving their arms at me to the beat; eyes already on stalks, maybe I was too late. I bopped my head and walked over, pretending to be into the music that sounded more like a calculator computing an equation than anything else. I joined their group and the two-step plodding began. We gave our usual ironic welcoming,

"Hey man, how's it going, man?" Introductions to plus ones and other friends were short, not too sweet.

It was time to get stuck in. I lifted my head and inhaled through my nose sharply while scanning the elongated narrow space we'd be in for the next seven hours; it was about to get interesting, surely.

Oh, it was.

Before I knew it, I was dancing with the lights and grinning as the music came to life. I felt like I could jive despite my usual detesting of any situation where I have to dance. My friends and I were in unison; passing brief gazes and smirks to one another as we collectively floated on the warehouse floor. The music still made little sense to me, but I stuck to the beat with as minimal effort as possible, step-lift-step and repeat. I was moving so smoothly. I had to appreciate the moment I was in; I had to savour this feeling. I turned to my left, my friends loving every minute as their wide eyes and sweaty foreheads shone in the light show; if only they could see themselves. I turned to the floor to examine my footwork, still going strong with the two-plodding; good work. I turned to my right and was immediately shocked at whom I'd found myself standing next to. My entire body shivered from head to toe. The surprise made my knees weak, it even broke my two-stepping. Directly to my right were three enormous fellow ravers, not particularly tall, but shaped like Greek gods. Every muscle on their body was defined as if sculpted by Michelangelo himself. Their bodies were exposed, except for chains in the shape of an X across their abdomens, connected round their necks. The sweat was bouncing off their bodies as they violently jerked to the beat, swinging their entire bodies with bone-crushing force, left shoulder, then right shoulder, as if they were possessed.

What were they on?

I peered forward to see the faces of these specimens, my curiosity once again dictating my behaviour. I begged myself not to stare, but I was fascinated. I've never seen somebody of such size move in that way. Back and forth they went with what seemed like an aggressive war dance, not a care for their surroundings. I looked past to see if anybody else was paying as much attention as I was, and that's when I noticed nobody cared but me. I was the minority at this event, stood in my long-sleeved navy t-shirt and hoodie still draping around my shoulders, surrounded by chains, latex, leather and more. They certainly weren't alone. I looked up towards the balcony that looped around the perimeter of the elongated room we stood in; even the stewards had masks on. Skulls, V for Vendetta/Guy Fawkes masks and balaclavas were all staring back at me from above. It felt like every eye was on me at this point and the walls were getting narrower. My chest began to rise as it filled with panic. My breath shortened and became sharper and my shoulders tensed forward. For the first time in my life, I felt claustrophobic, almost strangled, and needed air. I turned to my friends, who were all drooling with their eyes closed, also unfazed by their surroundings. I needed to breathe. I needed to get out.

I took a step to the side of my group and hid behind an enormous pillar, which blocked out enough of the thumping beat for me to think. For a couple of minutes I could focus on my breathing, slowing the sharp breaths into deeper inhales through my nose with a smooth blowing out through my mouth. My shoulders eased backwards and the panic from my chest slowly dropped off. I was back on cloud nine. I gazed over to where I'd been standing to get used to my surroundings, finding solace that there was still a sizeable minority in their flowery attire, sunglasses and glitter. This wasn't about them, or those half-naked in chains and leather, it was about spending time with my friends; this was fun.

I eased myself back over to my friends, most of who were in a different dimension to me. They were like Aztecs worshipping the Sun God, hailing the light display in front of them. Though I was with them, I couldn't shake the feeling that I was alone and out of place. I tried to enjoy the fact they were enjoying themselves and I was with them, but who wants to watch others have fun? One of our group approached me, giving me a light pat on my shoulder, his eyes like two black holes coming to swallow me.

"You alright, mate?" he asked with his ever gentle voice (if it's ever needed I want him to do my audiobook).

He's always been the caring one to check in on me and understands me not loving the music.

"Yeah, I'm good; floating man!"

Floating is what we would say in university to let each other know we were in a good space. It received the usual easy laugh and he put his arm round my shoulder,

"Love you, man," he told me, with a hopeless grin melted across his face.

"Love you too, man." I embraced him.

We both meant it, but it feels weird how the only time we can tell each other this is under the influence. It's good to let people know they're loved.

I met him one night in my first year of university; he'd been locked out of his apartment block after a night out, so threw stones at a window opposite to get some attention and ask for somewhere to stay. The window turned out to be mine. I recognised him from football trials, and though he'd woke me up at four in the morning. I said he could share my bed (the sofas in halls are like church benches). Despite the next morning feeling like a weird one-night stand, we've never looked back. I forever have the mick taken out of me from my first ever rave (Jurassic Park night), when I turned to him and declared how happy I was that he'd thrown stones at my window two years before. Pathetic.

Though his smile and his words were genuine in the warehouse, I was still light years away from where he was. His face appeared to be melting faster than a burning candle whereas I was still embarrassed to be nervous about people wearing chains and leather. I turned to my right again, curious as to how the Bane-like ravers were doing, this time I saw one of their faces. The jerking motions were still violent, as if they were in a trance, the same forceful thrusting of each shoulder with the beat. I gazed upon the closest person's face to see their eyes were not like my dear friends', whose eyes, by this point, could feature in a Stephen Hawking book. These eyes were filled with red cracks, with a red ring around the iris; I was starting to think they were possessed. They looked like robots being programmed in the way they moved. I felt another tap on my shoulder. Two of Hawking's black holes nodded in their direction.

"Meth heads."

I'm not sure if I'd ever come across anybody taking crystal meth, other than on *Breaking Bad*, which didn't depict it like this. Not that somebody claiming they were on meth makes it proof, but it was said with enough conviction that I believed it. I wasn't the only person with an eye on these three, glancing between them and the pretty lights, so pretty. As I turned back over from the pretty lights (they were so pretty), two of them gripped each other by the back of the head and began rolling their necks. The violence in their movement remained, the sweat still jumping from every defined muscle as they rocked side to side, before going in for the kill. They weren't just kissing, but biting too. Chomping. They were like two hippos fighting over a watermelon, and with it being 2018, I faced the front like a good boy. I didn't want to look like a creep who was made uncomfortable by what was happening two feet to my right. It was a bit too close and the violence in their movement did make me nervous. When the third person got involved with the kissing or biting, whatever it was, I knew I had to stop being curious and get on with enjoying myself. I inhaled until my lungs were full and looked up to the ceiling, which seemed miles away in this enormous warehouse. Lasers flew through the air above me. The music pounded into my chest and I tried to let go of feeling like I didn't belong there. It was in that moment as I looked up, all weight was lifted from me, any negative feeling I had was cast out and I knew this wasn't going to be my life.

I wasn't going to make appearances for the sake of pleasing others, I wasn't going to be at anybody's beck and call. I wasn't going to waste my time being somewhere I didn't want to be. I wasn't going to dress myself concerned about other people judging me. I'd figured something out. I thought about how I'm here for 80 years (hopefully) and there is no deep underlying meaning as to why I'm here, but I am, so I'm going to focus on me. I don't have to please other people if I don't want to. I became so overwhelmed, I welled up. My entire spine shivered to the point I had to roll my shoulders to absorb it (while the pretty lights shone through my tears, so pretty). I felt like I'd let go of everything. I closed my eyes.

I felt incredible, and I had to savour it. I've no idea how long I stood there with my eyes closed, it felt too long to be classed as a moment, but my golden moment of realisation was eventually interrupted with a tap on the shoulder. I turned to my left feeling almost god-like. Two black holes stared up at me and asked, "Can you get me a water please, mate? You're round."

Just like that, it was over.

"Yeah, course, I was about to get one anyway. Do you want anything else?"

Oh, piss off Andrew.

I remained still for a minute and scanned the world around me. It then dawned upon me, what was I doing? Not just here, at this rave, but in life; what was I doing? Why was I settled with such misery and keeping it locked inside but for moments like this? I didn't feel like the superhero of my movie, more an unnamed extra in the second scene, not even getting a line. I felt normal, underachieving, whatever you want to call it as the bright lights and thumping music disappeared. Then came those four words:

"You're really nothing special."

These four words haunt me because I am so desperate to be special. The comment came from a teacher in my secondary school about six months after I'd left for university. Though she hadn't taught me, she felt the need to tell a university friend of mine, who approached her asking if she knew me (crazy banter), that I thought I was clever but was, in fact, average and that I was "really nothing special". *Tell me what you really think.* We're all special in our own world. To be told I wasn't was crushing, no matter how I pretended to laugh it off. The worst part was that I barely knew her. Perhaps she was right and I am painfully normal as feared; maybe it was time to grow. "Can you get me a water please mate?" just like that, I was sucked back into the rave by the black holes. My eyes widened. I realised I had been two-stepping with my eyes closed again as I went back in time to being told I'm really nothing special. Probably was time for some fresh air and water.

Straight back to reality, twice in the space of a few minutes, but it wasn't so terrible; it's simply who I am. I'm not the kind of person to decline buying a friend a drink, especially a friend in a self-imposed need. I've no idea why, but in this strange period of my life, I realised my life isn't as bad as I thought. I needed to stop judging myself so harshly. There are far worse people than me and there are far better people than me. There is far worse going on than what surrounds me, and there is far better. I realised the need to accept myself and in turn be myself. Of course, people won't like me (we're about to get onto that), but I should be able to deal with it. I could cope with someone, whom I have no interest in, not liking me. It took 23 and a half years, but I'd found total solace in recognising who I am and that's all I need to be. I didn't ask to experience such a moment of self-discovery, I couldn't explain how the weight of the world bashed me over the back of the head in this moment at all, but it did. It was my epiphany. After my moment of reckoning I had a fantastic time. The lights danced with me and not even the sweaty meth heads could bother me as they ragged each other around (absolutely no issue with that at all, not even the slightest thought was given, none at all, ever).Nothing could upset me; I became untouchable and went to bed that evening still overcome at finding myself.

That was until the night terrors kicked in.

My dreams are often vivid. I wish my mind could give me a rest, particularly when I'm so fragile. The price of my imagination is having horrendous fears that own me, especially when I try to sleep. That night, I woke up having been locked in my cousin's house battling a shadowed spirit whom I've taken on before in my dream world. It's quite a horrific nightmare to experience, especially with the feeling of dream déjà vu. I lay cold in my bed, soaked from the sweat my petrified body released during my nightmare. I lay in the blackness with nothing but my thoughts; my worst enemy. I must have had less than four hours sleep, given it was still dark outside, but I was awake as ever, my mind too frightened to rest. All I could do was dwell. Having been so sure I'd figured myself out only hours ago, I lay there once again, second-guessing myself, *Surely I am a good person*, over and over in my head, begging myself for reassurance. I continued to lie there, thinking of every time I've inconvenienced or upset somebody – from the man who beeped and gesticulated towards me on the day I'd passed my driving test, for doing 29 in the right-hand lane of a 30 zone, to the lady who thought I'd made a tut in her direction at the salad bar at work, which made her turn around and apologise to me. If only she realised I was turning my nose up at the options available and not her taking far too long to select her own. I wish she knew that my eye-rolling was because I didn't want the chickpea and feta salad (hideous option, by the way). If only she knew the person I was.

Learning to accept who I am that day changed my life. Rather than drastically change my actions, I became more mindful of them, realising who I am. I try to live my life positively, not because I'm a great person, but through fear of making somebody else feel low like I've done at times. Living like this has had me engaging in small talk with too many strangers, but I know that listening to someone can make a huge difference. Despite me never wanting to talk to strangers, I will allow myself to converse with people I don't know for that reason. I have no idea what's going on in their life, so why would I risk upsetting them by being ignorant? This way of life has me labelled as a people pleaser, though why I'd kiss the backside of a 38-year-old mother of three at a family party for letting her show me pictures of a family holiday to Dubai, I'm unsure. I was always under the impression that brown-nosing was an act to get one something they wanted; a promotion or a Soho House membership. There's such a conflict in my mind, between being kind to people and fending off the aggressors in life (who ironically don't usually have much going on in theirs). The ability to bite my lip with the impatient and judgemental can be difficult, but it is something I believe everybody should do their best with; these people feed off nastiness. My finest example of keeping quiet was when a girl decided to tell her friends at a bar that I "love talking about myself so much" (I did enjoy writing this book) in an attempt to shame me. I kept quiet, though I was desperate to point out that she had two separate Instagram accounts dedicated to herself; something about a pot meeting a kettle? I could have brought it up but decided to laugh it off and say talking about myself was on my CV because I preferred the conversation be about me than her, obviously.

I can't always keep quiet though.

Her friends

It's only when I find myself deep into conversation with someone that I fall into the trap of my own annoying kindness, for I won't shoo anybody away without reason. Much like when I met some extended friends of EJ, who took an instant dislike toward me because they wanted her to get back with her ex-boyfriend, who was one of their own. They called me the usual Scouse so-and-so banter. I know partner's friends and family are supposed to judge us harshly, but they can at least be reasonable. Her extended friends are four years my senior, as EJ is. We'd recently started seeing each other and on a night out, one of her friends swanned up to me to brand me as 'skinny' in front of her, in an attempt to put me down. Big man. In fact, he was too big. His stomach was so large that it popped open his third button from the bottom of his shirt, which I couldn't resist pointing out. Surprisingly this was quite the conversation killer for him. However, I'd continue to find myself in conversation with these alpha-mentality super-lads due to their persistent protection of their friend, like brothers protecting a younger sister. How admirable. As a side note, I can't stand it when people use the term 'alpha'. Aren't people who use the term alpha to describe their behaviour not a natural alpha by definition, as they have to consciously think about behaving in a certain way? Eventually, for the sake of getting peace on my nights out with EJ, I allowed myself to converse with her friends, at which point they made their judgement upon me. One of them put his arm around me on the final ever university night out and said, "You know, you're actually alright, mate."

Spare me. To think that I give such idiots airtime in an attempt to be judged as being 'actually alright', as if I'm looking for their acceptance. Do me a favour. I'd rather be cussed at and abused, than for someone – particularly whom I am engaging with at someone else's request – to tell me that I am actually a reasonable person to talk to. I hate it.

I know I'm great fun. Only a select few remain in contact with EJ and they're much the nicer of the group.

Fast forward three and a half years and I was still getting judged by her friends, this time it was one of her gals, her Prosecco prinnies, her sassy cats. I much prefer drunk honesty from her lady friends, one of whom decided to tell me how lucky I was to be with EJ having lived with her for a year at this point, to which I responded, "No, she's pretty lucky to be with me really," in a flippant, cocky manner.

I realised this is not an appropriate joke to tell to a woman who's been glugging Prosecco for eight hours, because alcohol drastically shortens people's temper and rational thinking. Her response to me was, "You're just a cunt, you're so nasty."

At least when swearing at me, I knew that she wasn't trying to patronise me or give me a certain kind of false approval. Luckily I had no interest in her opinion of me (it was post-epiphany) so just laughed and carried on with my life, waiting for her apology, which came on Facebook Messenger (which people apparently still used after 2014) a week and a half later.

Her friends are my friends.

I have no idea of why people feel the need to weigh in and judge on friendships or relationships that do not concern them. Thankfully, my own friends wouldn't dream of passing comment towards EJ, not because they're better people galloping around on their high horses, but because they're a bang-average group of twentysomething boys, definitely not men, who don't care. They couldn't care less about the minutiae of my relationship. They just don't want to be the first to propose to their girlfriends. It couldn't be more opposite when my girlfriend gets with her lot, she'll open up and tell them that I don't want to return to Sheffield, her home town because I attended university there and want to leave it behind me, but she isn't sure about Liverpool as she has no connections there. It's all a bit much to discuss with your gals after a day of drinking in my opinion. On the other hand, my friends and I rarely discuss our lady companions, we're usually just glad to be away from them in our own world, which surprisingly doesn't involve discussing our girlfriends and how lucky we are to be with them (I'd never admit it but I can't even sleep without EJ anymore). Perhaps we'll discuss the living dynamics, given that there's still a novelty about it to us; being newly moved in. Predominantly, we're in the stage of the relationship where all we want is peace, so will allow ourselves to be walked all over by our lady-companions in order to get time with our own friends and be left alone to have a drink in peace without getting texts asking where we are. It doesn't take long at all after moving in together.

I appreciate its human nature to pass judgement on others; we do it without thinking most of the time. There are two clear paths that we must choose from as we delve into judging other people. Firstly, the darkened path, in which we walk up to said person or people, whom I'll now refer as the 'subject', and let them know about how we've perceived them to be, thus criticising their character or behaviour. Realistically, we never positively judge people in our minds. Saying what we think directly to others isn't a brave move to make, nor is it admirable. Those who can't keep their opinions to themselves and believe their own words to be gospel, typically follow this path. The philosophy of 'telling it like it is' doesn't make anybody a beacon of integrity that all of society should look up to; rather it makes them unwanted from most conversations.

On the other hand, there is the more dignified path of judgement, one where those who have the ability to control their emotions and keep their opinions away from the subject. Whatever you call it – being two-faced, slagging off, bitching – it's enjoyable and definitely healthy in small doses (I was taught that in the second year of my medical training). It is far better for a person to wilfully fight the urge to pass harsh criticism on to another and instead wait to tell a friend or family member behind closed doors. We can sit in the comfort of our own home for hours slating and slamming people for their actions and it's undoubtedly the healthier way to live. It means that not only does the conversation between those in the room never dry up, but also the subject being berated does not become upset with us. However, immense caution is required when taking this path. I always begin with the enormous caveat of, 'Don't say anything', which is a much shortened version of me begging those listening to me to not spread my words of resentment, I'm casually saying, 'Please never repeat this, I'm too scared for them to find out and the consequences it may bring.' I'm aware nobody keeps a secret; there is absolutely zero chance that what I say about other people is not repeated. If I had a mortgage (ha ha good one), I'd bet the entirety of it on any time I've begun a conversation with 'don't say this', it has been repeated by everybody listening.

Why are we so useless?

No matter how much I stress the need for confidence, I know with any secret I tell, the person I'm talking to will spend the entire conversation deciding who they can tell. In turn, the person they tell has to act like they've not heard it before when I discuss it with them at a later point in time. People acting like they haven't heard something before is telling, yet I too have to buy into the façade so they're convinced I have no suspicion they already know what I'm telling them. Eventually, there will be a moment when the person you are confiding in can't keep the secret that another friend has already told them three weeks before. In which case the whole conversation is rendered pointless. Again, we're useless. As a result, I can't trust any of my best friends with as much as a crisp packet.

I accept I'll be judged, sometimes justified, other times not, but that's part of life. I make a conscious decision to ignore judgement from those not in my friendship circle, unless it comes from those who take the darkened path and say it to my face, then it's difficult. One of the things I'm judged on is that my dad has earned his living as a solicitor; how this has any bearing on me I'll never know. Of course, I'm grateful for the position I'm in, we're lucky enough just to be alive, never mind having what I see to be a privileged life. But it doesn't come without endless judgement. From being called a posh twat my entire childhood; to the assumptions my siblings and I went to a private secondary school, something I'm delighted I didn't because I'd be tenfold the arsehole I am. There's quite a misunderstanding about some people's relationships in families and how money is exchanged. One summer, my sister's best friend of 15 years, said to her, "Surely your dad can pay for you to visit me in Miami."

As if he'd just send her to Miami without a thought. He could have, obviously, and did offer. However, she couldn't go because she didn't want to.

The leg up in life

There's a time and a place to discuss other people's situations, ideally behind each others' backs; family parties certainly aren't the place. So I thought. It was a typical case of an introvert getting brave after fuelling their confidence with alcohol. I returned home-home late on a Friday night after another miserable week in the capital. I couldn't go to my house, rather straight to a bar, where my cousin's ukulele band was playing his birthday gig. By his band I mean he's the bassist of the quartet. The whole of my mum's side of the family had decided to go and support him; they're great for things like that. Nobody ever watched me play football though. I strolled in late to see every person in my family pretty drunk from their four or so hours of drinking together. One auntie had told her husband to piss off, my dad's left eye had firmly closed over and my granddad was dancing like a drunk granddad at his grandson's gig. I dived straight into a game of catch-up.

It didn't take long for the drink and fatigue to catch up with me. I became ever more reliant on resting on the bar to stand up and was becoming part of the furniture myself when the girlfriend of a cousin's friend (I think) approached me. I'd met her once previously and she barely uttered a word, so I had no informed opinion of her. When she walked over, I asked how she was, like any normal person would do. She said she was good, but instead of returning the pleasantry, she told me she'd just been telling my parents that she felt I'd had a certain "leg up in life", that she had not been given. Okay. Again, this was in response to my question asking how she was. Wish I hadn't asked. Friday night. I believe people can genuinely make mistakes in being rude, even without realising they're doing so, such as accusing somebody they've met once beforehand that they've had everything handed to them in life. I also believe that I've had an easy ride in life compared to many, I'd be a fool to not think so, but I've still worked hard (if you want proof, I passed both my theory and practical driving tests first time). So I gave her a chance and attempted to deflect her remark to avoid jumping into the risky rabbit hole we stood at the edge of, but my effort was in vain. The girlfriend continued to accuse me of being privileged like I was somehow in denial, or in the wrong for being born. I was also wrongly accused of voting for a certain political party and wrongly accused of having my university tuition paid for. I just wanted another beer (paid for by my dad).

I'd worked hard at some point that week.

A time I am quick to judge anybody is if they're quick to introduce family backgrounds or politics into a conversation, given that nobody really discusses religion, particularly after a drink. I detest discussing political views almost as much as I detest talking about my job, powder, even if it is pure powder and hypothetical football conversations. Nobody cares how many goals and assists Lionel Messi would get if he played for Manchester United and not Barcelona his entire career. If anybody talks family situations or politics at a gathering, they ought to take themselves off and hop into the nearest bin for the evening. Time and place. I've no idea why she tried to call out my family life like that. why would somebody say that? It's not like my family are swinging from the branches of the Rothschild family tree and laughing at the poor, setting fire to money in front of the homeless. My parents were from working-class families and my dad became a solicitor, he's hardly Bill Gates. Here I am, years later feeling the need to justify it to you; is that through fear of being judged?

It's events as such that I'll obsess over, replaying scenarios in my head, wishing that I'd not allowed myself to be judged and misjudged, such is the curse of heightened self-awareness. How I wish to be free. If I'd have corrected her on my political vote, or about my university tuition, then she'd have judged me as better in her eyes, but that would have involved me justifying myself towards that person; would that be enabling them? This is why I can never sleep, this and being scared of the dark.

Judge me on my results

Between university and working in London, I've seen my fair share of people desperately trying to grab onto the ladder of success. We all want to be the boss, cruising between meetings, eating the best food paid for by clients and being hated by our employees as we watch the money pile into our banks. None of us have an idea of how to get there, it's a guessing game, all we can do is work hard and hope for the best. Though my initial guess is that wearing shirts and shoes to university lectures isn't going to make you succeed, but who am I to say what succeeding is? Moving to the ambition capital of the world, I realised how desperate people were to become a success story; changing the way they dressed, spoke and behaved in an attempt to give people a better impression of themselves. Why not be yourself? Graduate inductions are a goldmine for the false. False confidence, false interests, false attitudes; it's all a façade at a graduate induction.

My induction in September 2016 was particularly dull. On day one of my financial job in London, we, a room of over 500 fresh-faced graduates, were given an introductory talk from a top partner at the firm discussing the day-to-day life of financial analysis and how being committed to their clients was integral to everything they do. It wasn't the most inspiring of speeches. I wouldn't compare it to Al Pacino's war cry in *Any Given Sunday*. It was more a brief introduction with us sitting politely and fighting the urge to fall asleep in a dimly lit and warm conference room. As the speech came to a close, the speaker asked if we had any questions. As most who are 90 minutes into a job, during which they've experienced only a lecture about life at the firm, I had none. I wanted to get my free laptop and go home for the afternoon, ready to become a billionaire, baby. The hands shot up around me; clearly I was not as prepared as others in the room.

"What's the most difficult thing you've worked on?"

A classic vacant question, asked by someone who wants to ask a question for its sake, despite it not benefitting anybody in the room. Thankfully, this partner wasn't egotistical and she gave a very concise, polished answer that basically said, "I'm not going to go into detail."

Yet for some reason, following the answer to the question, the loudmouth responded with, "Thank you for the answer."

What? Thanking someone for responding to a question? Rubbish. A second hand was called upon to ask a question.

"Thank you very much for your speech, it was really interesting and insightful. Have you always been at the firm and how has your role changed as you have progressed?"

I remember this well, word for word (fine, you got me). It was the opening line that threw me. I turned to my right in shock as to how anybody could find it interesting. Surely that was brown-nosing? The boy next to me muttered, "fucking hell" under his breath. He's now a good friend, who too is regularly impersonated for his soft Glaswegian accent, though those mimicking him make him sound like he lives in a shopping trolley under a bridge in Aberdeen.

We both bonded through our mutual judgement of the trolls who piped up with their subservient remarks to the partner, begging to be recognised. They were asking abysmal questions as well. They must have been told that asking questions from a crowd of over 500 people would get them remembered. They weren't wrong, a classic LinkedIn profiler move.

What is a LinkedIn profiler?

Earlier in the book I mentioned those who enjoy talking too much about their job. Similarly, LinkedIn profilers are those who go through life with networking and work always on their mind, focusing on becoming the next success story. Grow the network and grow the chance of success. In an ideal world, yes, every moment of our career would be fruitful, giving us a better understanding and bettering ourselves, or the world in some way. LinkedIn profilers live in this fantasy world, where every conversation could lead to an advantage at some point in their career. Every conversation comes with excessive effort for no other reason than to be a memorable face should they reach out in the future. Their forced interest and conversation can be felt from miles away because it is so false; it's difficult to ignore. What happened to being ourselves? (This shouldn't be confused with my professional self. Remember him, whose role is to stop me from crying every 22 minutes in the office?)

It's too easy to pass judgement on these people. It's like conversing with a shop window selling its services. They're willing to bombard you with heaps of information about themselves in a short time frame. They're particularly infuriating outside of work. When I'm away from Canary Wharf, the crown jewel of the successful mindset, I like to think about anything but my employer, such is the dismal life in financial services. However, they could talk for hours about their professional lives, what they read (never 'studied') at university, where they had sex, what they do for day-to-day work, how many drinks they can drink in one night and function the next day. See you in Infernos, you legend. All the while we must pretend to be enthused by the conversations they've forced upon us, plenty of head-nodding so we look like we're listening when in reality, I'll stand there planning an escape route. At least with work drinks, the drinks are free, so I can justify putting up with it, but when I'm out trying to enjoy my free time, it saddens me being trapped by Captain Driven.

As I said, it's too easy to judge LinkedIn profilers we don't know. Judgement carries greater weight with those we choose to surround ourselves with, particularly when money gets involved.

Money money money

Money is the ultimate tool for judgement. Why is money such a taboo topic that people act strangely around? We have varying levels of income and different family backgrounds that we were born into, but that doesn't hold any influence on relationships, or at least it shouldn't. I'm unsure of the dictionary definition of each class, but if I had to class myself, I'd assume I was raised as a middle-class child, hence my decision to move to London to chase money in financial services and retire at the age of 35; what a naïve cretin. I went to a state school in Liverpool where I learned to value any shred of privilege I had. I'd learn to value aspects of my life that seemed a given at the time, like having parents who are still married, because I had classmates who had their school meals paid because their single parent was struggling to raise a family. My friendship group has a wide range of backgrounds, which did not affect our relationship growing up, but as soon as we started earning our own money it became an absolute shambles.

The biggest bane of any friendship is the flow of money. Nothing infuriates members of a group quite like when you're out for the day buying drinks and one person in the group is a round-dodger. In every group, there will be the frontrunners, the early birds who are happy to get the first or second drink in. They trust their companions to return the favour without issue. Following the frontrunners, there are the reliable-returners; not usually the first to put their hands in their pocket, but they are without doubt contributing, just as the drinks start flowing that bit quicker and the group settles into the round-buying. Yet there is always a round-dodger, who thinks if they leave it long enough, their round will disappear into thin air; it'll be lost in time and space. They grip the penultimate drink in the round for so long, slowing down so they appear to be incapable of keeping up with the rest of the group, despite having five drinks beforehand without issue. Those in the round become too impatient to wait, so head for the bar to quench the thirst; such is the way with alcohol. The dodger will refuse the new drink, knowing that they can't get away with it a second time. They have run out of free drinks so must remain quiet until they get a moment to slip away. The drink in their hand lasts an awfully long time as the round continues to pick up pace and the memories become a little patchy. When the time is right, the dodger slips away to get another drink, maybe disguised with a toilet trip. Off they worm to the bar having had a full round of free drinks, justifying it in their own heads that they cannot waste their funds on buying drinks for their friends.

In the absence of any confusion, everybody knows a round-dodger's game and who the dodgers are; it never goes unnoticed. It's a terrible trait to have, though some people hate spending money so much they're satisfied with being branded as tight among even their best of friends, who, of course, will never refuse to buy them a drink. What else are friends for? It just takes one brave soul of the pack to call out the cheat for their actions and it soon changes; it did for my group. We can now split bills and buy rounds in peace, it may still irritate the coin counter of the group, but it's the fairest thing to do. I put my confidence in the law of averages.

This attitude, which has carried me through my young adult life, has led to my closest friends judging me. I'll constantly have to laugh off jibes from others about me being spoiled, having an easy life, and having everything handed to me, though it's far from the case. Yet I have to take it with a smile on my face because compared to most I have lived in comfort. How could I not be bothered by it? I'm not looking for sympathy, merely expressing my disliking for the unjustified labelling, for making jokes about money, with people missing the obvious irony that I'm on a graduate salary (plus subsidised rent, I know, I know). People don't know my situation really, even if they think they do. Perhaps I shouldn't judge so much after all, or maybe I should get my parents to buy me an ivory tower to cry in and judge from the top of. That could make me feel better and means they wouldn't have to help with rent anymore.

In making a decision we assess the options we have and act accordingly, hoping for the best possible outcome – be it accepting a job offer, asking somebody out on a date, choosing what cereal to buy, or whether it's worth risking a fart, it's part of our nature. But this human trait is magnified on social media when others' judgement is forced into our lives every time we open an app. It has a much longer-lasting print than somebody telling their friends in a bar that you love yourself, even if that's not entirely true. Through social media, everybody has bought into the false notion that their opinion is as important to everybody as it is to themselves. People have become harsher and more outrageous with their opinions and judgement to gain traction on social media to make themselves feel better. A negative reaction is better than no reaction. With the recent combination of the globalisation of human communication and the political correctness movement, it hasn't taken long to land in our current climate. We're now, according to anybody over the age of 35, the generation of the offended, who seem to have no better way to spend our free time than to complain about advertising campaigns, product labels, tweets, or even comedy – the art form that provides joy. There's an element of truth in this, though I disagree that anybody born in the 90s onwards is a mentally weak worm. Nevertheless, some search down the crevices of mainstream media, hoping to find offence and broadcasting it over the internet.

Giving us all a bad name.

Chapter VII – Hi, I'm offended, nice to meet you

Life's a struggle, it really is. It's draining. People are draining, commuting is draining, work is draining, being kind is exhausting, socialising is draining, being healthy is draining. It's a constant uphill battle and that's for someone without any real problems. Boredom is the worst of all. If I'm bored, I feel like I'm waiting to die, so I force myself to be active and make commitments I don't want to make, or journeys I don't want to take, just so I don't sit around being bored, waiting to die. I see seemingly better situations to mine regularly through various forms of media and am constantly made to feel like I'm missing out on something great to a point where I'm made to feel anxious for how mediocre I am. Yet I can't moan about this life without being told I'm soft, told I'm lacking some real struggle in my life, like digging a ten-feet deep trench to avoid being shelled by The Bosh, or being blind. I'm told that I'm part of the snowflake generation, usually by people in their forties, fifties and sixties, who funnily enough didn't experience the second world war, so I'm unsure as to why they refer to it like they were there. It's not our fault we were born 50 years after Hitler died. Surely I'm allowed to moan while getting on with my life.

The truth is I am, yes.

I'm allowed to moan freely about my gripes with life, but I have to recognise that if I'm to moan people will challenge me, as they are free to. Although, I couldn't imagine not being thoughtful and respectful of how others feel when I spoke. I suppose that's thanks to activists who've come before me and whom I've learned from. As a 24-year-old, I cannot fathom judging somebody for anything other than their personality and actions because of those who have stood out and stood up in the past to challenge true injustices in society and change the public's attitude to racism, anti-Semitism, sexism, homophobia as well as the many other forms of discrimination and oppression. I've not done anything ground-breaking myself to personally challenge these notions, I just cannot imagine not seeing any other person as my equal (other than those who call people from Liverpool 'bin-dippers', they're rubbish humans). I'm lucky to be in a society that has zero tolerance towards the above issues; well, it's supposed to.

There are still huge problems faced by minority groups across the world. African-Americans battle with police and their government over police brutality, where African-Americans are shot dead by white police officers; murdered for no other reason than being black. In Russia, as recently as 2014, a bill was passed to criminalise 'gay propaganda', making it illegal to promote LGBTQ+ equality in a country where people can be physically harmed just for their race and sexual orientation. A 16-year-old named Maxim Neverov was prosecuted and fined in 2018 as a result of posting pictures of men on his social media account. Fined for being gay; that's insanity (this was later resolved in a court appeal). Only it isn't, these are real problems, incredible injustices that huge numbers of people face, but we can't all relate to them, as many of us don't experience these injustices. This isn't to say that it doesn't happen in the UK; there are still gross levels of discrimination.

I believe it is because many are without these struggles to our basic fundamental freedoms, that people go in search of meaningless things they find offensive to cause a stir, or make a tweet go viral and get some attention. The majority of people are completely content with going about their daily lives, channelling their efforts into making a better life for themselves and others, however that might be.

However, a tiny proportion of the population go about their lives seeking to disagree with others and to claim offence has been caused toward them because they crave the attention that isn't being given to them. These people are merely attention seekers, who believe any attention is good for them. Kind of like a newspaper. That's why they abuse celebrities to get a reaction or fabricate stories to gather traction or promote distasteful views to shock people engaging with social media. It's all an attempt to boost clicks to their profile. It's a numbers game, which is how the likes of Katie Hopkins have managed to thrive. At least she took the risk of competing on *The Apprentice* (for which the standard of contestant has drastically gone downhill, but we need not dwell on that) to demonstrate her skill set before she became a public figure spreading vulgar opinions.

It is all for the sake of attention because receiving attention makes people happy. However, offence-seekers seem to misinterpret somebody clicking 'like' on a comment of theirs with true fanaticism or credit for work they've created. They manage to get their dopamine feed solely from that, which realistically shows the level they're at. Attention seekers and trolls have no financial gain from being talked about on the latest Discover page, they're just begging for attention and will go to bizarrely low standards to get it. Why can't they get a hobby? They could do something creative like burying their thoughts in a book for a couple of years instead. It hurts nobody (as nobody's reading these books, let's be honest) and would probably make them feel accomplished to a degree.

In October 2018, one tweet from a mother went viral (no doubt she worked at Full Time Mum on her Facebook profile). She was outraged that a tissue company had labelled their brand of large tissues as 'Mansize'. This time-wasting chump published her own short story, telling that her child aged four asked if "boys, girls and mummies" could use the tissues as well, then demanding that the company change the name of the box to something more appropriate (which they did, so at least it was a success story). This was done for absolutely no reason other than she was probably bored. Her exact reasoning was, "It is 2018". For the avoidance of any doubt, attached was a photo of the box as evidence. This is the perfect example of faux-feminism that exists, particularly in mainstream media. This tweet did end up in the press, who used it to joke how far feminism has come, thus opening an enormous can of worms, such as men asking if a TV show being called '*Loose Women*' was then sexist (do us all a favour mate and delete your social media). I've encountered a faux-feminist myself, in work, when a friend I was walking with held the door for a lady no more than two yards behind us. Holding the door is no act of chivalry; it's politeness we are taught as a child in school. It's on par with saying 'please' and 'thank you', which funnily enough, is a welcomed response for holding the door open for someone. However, when the door was held for this middle-aged woman, she commented, "Holding it for a woman, you're too kind."

Being 30 years younger, he bit his tongue, most likely through fear of getting sacked for saying anything to her. He had to settle for an elongated stare into my soul, as I offered nothing back but pressing both my lips together and raising my eyebrows to my (ever-rising) hairline.

These political correctness fanatics, who long for a sanitized world of nothingness, do exist in a minority, but they cast an incredibly large shadow for their size. This is solely down to the outrageousness of their claims, not the validity of them. Accusations of being sexist stick, but when somebody insinuates you're sexist for holding a door open it's pathetic. They're both real examples of the effect these offence-seeking time wasters have, that holding a door open seems like a macho aggressive action. I doubt these women were asked to feature in James Cameron's *Titanic*, imagine if a man had told them that women and children could leave the boat first. They'd have each picked up a violin and gone down with the orchestra so women weren't undermined. We don't need their stupidity in the gene pool anyway. Such views (and they are absolutely not alone) do more to degrade activism than to empower it, particularly due to the media's attitude to picking up stories, such as the tissue tantrum, and broadcasting it in mockery, at the expense of all women. Feminism is in another realm to this profanity, as are most, but this toxic world of offence-seeking has given rise to an even worse group of people – the Meninists – just when you thought it couldn't get more ridiculous.

I wish this was part of a joke.

While offence-seekers trawl through the internet, in the real world, the views that have previously placed only white men in powerful, high-earning roles are slowly being challenged. Just six of Britain's FTSE100 companies have female CEOs, as of the end of 2018 and five people who aren't white, fewer than the number of white CEOs called Steve, remember. Despite these statistics, there's the new breed of online trolls, who feel the need to campaign for white men's rights as they feel they're being discriminated against. They (pretend to) believe that men are now the enemy of the 21st century because they're made fun of in adverts, or gender pay gaps are published to show evidence of how skewed society is in favour of men; white men to be specific. They're a tiny minority of men, but once again they are persistent with their social media because they've got nothing better to do than sit on their phone and argue, begging for somebody to snap at their senseless opinions. If women want to empower each other online, it hasn't exactly got much to do with me. I just keep scrolling (looking for dog content), as it doesn't affect my life. But there will always be a Brian – whose Twitter display picture is Popeye, post-spinach, with a football tattoo on his forearm, with a bio that reads 'electrician, fried chicken lover, football fan, part-time musician, full-time Meninist' – who has tweeted 27,000 times despite having 73 followers, and his response will read, 'Why just women? Why not empower all[5] people?' These people actually exist.

Again, this segment of society is small in numbers, but through their favourite hobby of scanning the internet and social media, they make an awful lot of noise. The vast majority of us sane folk are left to witness an historic war of petulant name-calling and attention-begging through the social media battlefield, or the comments on the *Daily Mail* website. I don't read them myself but the odd picture has been shared my way; it is a goldmine for the pathetic. We're unable to steer clear of this war, for the extremes are used as mainstream clickbait. A headline that causes outrage will always get people reading, no matter how nonsensical. As I mentioned before, we now live under the false notion that our opinions are worth more to the world than basic facts. This statement couldn't apply more to a group of people than those in the trenches of the political correctness war.

Where does this end? We've seen that some public figures have forged careers on making controversial statements that tow incredibly close to (far beyond) the line of what is responsible to say in society. Fake news stories are spread widely and there's little way for those reading them to understand what is even remotely true. People also seem

---

5. The utterly depressing point is that I wrote this in late 2018. During my time editing this book (as you may have noticed this was completed just before the beginning of 2020), the Black Lives Matter movement was met with the same people asking, 'Why don't all lives matter?' Imagine being that desperate for attention.

to forget that ultimately, you're reading somebody else's opinion. I believe every news outlet has its own agenda, be it to please investors, promote political stances, or to get people clicking on their pages while they take a 20-minute poo at three o'clock in the afternoon to steer clear from their desk for as long as possible. We have allowed this content to riddle our society like cancer spreading through the blood.

All we want from social media is a quick break from our lives, but instead of being entertained, we're told how to think, reminded of better places we could be, who said what, and where they said it. Opinions from all sides of any argument are vilified and we can often be belittled just from what we see online. It is those who are upset when others don't agree with their opinion, those who cannot debate intelligently with the opposite side, who spread this story of everybody being easily offended, that are offended by everything themselves. These people shut down any opinion that isn't their own and jump onto tangents to promote their own argument. This hostile environment makes people think there's no point in discussing how they feel or any opinion they have because they don't want the hassle of being branded ignorant, a fool, or being called a snowflake.

There's more to this.

In a previous chapter, I discussed the medium of targeted advertising; algorithms ran by faceless companies that track every click and move we make online. Every move is saved to our online profile like scar tissue. Any purchase we make is stored, its details are analysed and then compared with thousands upon thousands of other details stored online and these algorithms will match certain products to shove in our direction. Remember the little book of Trumpisms and the cap that I'm still paying the price for two years on? It runs far deeper than what we purchase. Our details have been sold to the highest bidders without our knowledge, all because we read an article about which breed of dinosaur we'd be, based on a questionnaire. We receive scores of harassing emails per day of new venues to eat food, new activities to do with our friends, holidays to go on, what clothes we should be interested in, festivals to attend and bars to drink at. It's a never-ending bombardment in a life ultimately dominated by media and clever technology. I'd guess this to be the root of the generation's heightened anxieties and frets and not because we're naturally weaker for not growing up in the aftermath of a world war, or the war itself. We're the generation ruled by numbers. Our privacy has been traded between companies that we've never contacted based on their advertising agreements with companies we engage with, thousands of times.

We're milked for any spare cash we have because a company can spend next to no cash on maintaining automated email systems that churn out daily nonsense about the latest thing we absolutely cannot miss out on. We are constantly harassed. Just because there's no human being poking us and asking for our money doesn't excuse the fact that we are harassed. I booked my final flight with a notoriously poor airline in April 2018, roughly 40 days before I flew with some friends to Portugal. Unfortunately for me, they had the most convenient flight times that allowed me to leave work just before three in the afternoon, thus not taking a day of official annual leave. It's a classic ploy. I was left with the choice of take the day off or book with them. Within ten minutes of booking my flight, I'd received confirmation, a second email recommending hotels for me to stay in and a third one showing me car rental prices. Naturally, having planned my weekend to the point all I needed was a flight, I ignored the emails and carried on about my day, sifting through the other 50 emails to get rid of so that the red icon on my phone would vanish and I'd feel like I had nothing to answer. In the

40 days that led up to the flight, I received 36 emails about optional extras and additional bookings with my flight; at least a quarter of which were about pre-booking a seat for £8. This may sound like spiel plucked from One Hundred Tales of a Hypochondriac, but the reality is that my generation, the snowflakes, those trying to get on with their lives without interference are finding it impossible to do so. We can't turn off any emails, or messages, they play too vital a part in society. We can't even block these advertisers because they forward the same messages through what seems like infinite addresses. Yes, I've clicked unsubscribe before.

The older generations cannot understand this level of annoyance from their teenage years onwards. They have always known that their life behind closed doors was private. We naively invited thousands of people, companies and institutions into our homes and now we can't get rid of them. They're with us every night and we must acknowledge them at least. The technological revolution that's defined, particularly the last decade, has been a breeding ground for harassment, hostility and as a result, constant fear. Here's another example of how times have changed. Before this past decade, going out for drinks with friends (we're not going back into the Instagram fools, don't worry) would end when the bars closed and it was time to head home. There was little chance of making a fool of one's self when making the trip home. The most people could hope to look at was a ripped piece of paper showing a scribbled house number on it, which belonged to someone they chatted with. How simple that must have been.

Now we have the opportunity to both harass and be harassed (obviously you have to be weird to harass somebody), without having to lift more than our scrolling thumb. We are able to gain a huge amount of detail without even having to make an effort. All we need is a name and we have access to somebody's online persona: phone number for calling, texting and WhatsApp; Instagram account; Facebook account; Twitter account; Snapchat and all the other apps we can use for dating and communication. Couple that with six or seven hours of binge drinking and it can really be more than a sore head in the morning. We've learned the detrimental effects phones have on our brains that release dopamine every time our phone gets a notification (it's true, I saw it on a YouTube video). Similarly, there's an overwhelming feeling of dread when we wake up from a drunken night as we tear through every app possible, praying we haven't drunk-dialled, texted, liked or anything else without remembering; because it makes us feel creepy. It seems so insignificant, even reading this paragraph, but the fretting caused when you realise you did send that person you had sex with six months ago a random message at four in the morning. No response, obviously. Unless it's just a sympathy 'ha ha', if they're kind enough (obviously this hasn't happened to me in the last six years, or ever).

What about the recipients of such messages? We can't help but feel flattered when we get any messages, but drunk messages make us feel like someone is thinking about us in the early hours, though it absolutely is influenced by alcohol, drugs, or both and in no way like a romantic comedy fantasy that we fool ourselves into thinking about for days following. We can't help but feel that way. I'd never accuse anybody who has sent me a drunk message to be harassing me, mainly because I received so few I was grateful to get any. But if this goes on for an extended period of time, does it become harassment? There are only so many times one can turn another person down in the name of love, yet there are many opportunities available to their ambitious counterparts.

Generations before us who've danced into the early hours cannot fathom these lingering dreads, for they've never experienced this cesspool of madness that is the connected world. A world where a few taps of a screen, no matter if we believe it to be in jest, can ruin the relationships we have and our world around us. If only we believed in a universal philosophy that these microscopic digital messages, which are nothing more than a series of codes, were trivial and more of a parody of ourselves than potentially being harmful and offensive interactions. It's almost too simple for us to completely ruin ourselves, especially as everything is recorded and engraved into our digital footprint, which does not wash away like those where sand meets water. Every message, like and click is stored and there's nothing we can do about it. This subconscious worry is nothing like ever experienced by those before us. They cannot imagine being in a taxi heading home in the early hours, armed with Dutch courage and asking the taxi driver to take them to the home of the person whose number they'd received that night (first they'd have to obtain it from an address book, they'd be asleep by the time they'd opened the contents page) and if by this small miracle the taxi driver complied with their wish to take them to said address, what would they do? They wouldn't get out of the car, climb up the side of the house and double tap on their lover's bedroom window, blurting out, 'I liked the way you looked on your summer holiday! Yes, the one that was seven months ago, the picture you took wearing the yellow top was really something; love heart eyes emoji.'

Even if this wholly unlikely event did occur, the sleeping lover being harassed wouldn't be notified and would in theory never know. The drunkard would be saved from the embarrassment, and not want to die the next morning. It would all be swept under a weighty rug for nobody to see, completely forgotten. Not for us, not even close, every click and comment is logged and notifies the recipient. They don't need to be awake, everything we say can be there waiting for them in the morning. Even if we manage to delete the messages, likes or comments in time, the notifications still get sent for them to wake up to; great isn't it? Every morning that follows an evening drinking we must spend scouring all forms of contact possible, praying that we haven't said anything, liked any incriminating pictures that show the world our drunken desires, which, by the way, are nothing more than the alcohol flowing through us. If you don't believe that then you probably don't have enough to drink.

I'm fortunate to not feel the need to discuss my feelings through the medium of social media with my followers when sober or drunk. Firstly, even in the drunkest of states, I'm well aware that those who follow me only do so out of mutual politeness. They follow me, so I'll follow them as long as they're not hyperactive. This is to increase their number of followers, or that they think I'm attractive so don't have a real interest in what I have to say anyway; that's how it works, isn't it? But for some, however, they feel the need to post their opinions when drunk, which, much like the messages to our drunken love interests, are not deleted, ever. Even if you think you have deleted it in time, I can guarantee there is someone who has seen the content you've generated and saved an image of your little creation.

I'll never forget a teammate in the university football team, who tweeted "[Insert girl's full name], where are you?" There was extensive use of question and exclamation marks, and the fact it was time-stamped at 3.45 am gave the game away. He deleted the tweet, but by the time I'd woken up I'd received saved pictures of the tweet in two different group chats. The anxiety it must have caused the next day would have been crippling, particularly as he'd only slept with her once. I don't think it went much further afterwards. Older generations may say, 'don't take the phone with you, we didn't', but that's ridiculous. We're now in a world where we must carry phones as an extension of our own bodies to remain connected. Sure, if Simon Cowell, millionaire producer with mass influence doesn't want to use a phone, that's great for him. He doesn't need to remain connected when he's had a full career, enormous wealth and started a family. Small businesses, employees, people creating their own content, we all need to remain connected, for now at least, while our new life online is still in its adolescence.

So how does all of this affect an average person of the generation who's offended?

Chapter VIII – Triggered

The event

The constant low levels of fretting cause us to feel increasingly vulnerable whether we recognise this or not. Our vulnerability makes it difficult to cope with major and potentially damaging events, which I've learned are referred to as triggers. I don't mean being vexed at a film advert on the side of a London bus that ironically says 'Men are like buses…' but when we undergo a true state of panic or stressful event. Our constant mild apprehensions quickly turn into anxieties that take over our lives and lead to ill mental health. That's why I believe it's so prominent now; not just the fact that more people are open about it, but that we all have a raised average level of anxiety that means we're easily affected by events surrounding us.

Here is mine. I wish this wasn't true. It's so embarrassing. I've always hated going to sleep as I have an irrational fear of the dark. I hate the silence of night. My dreams have haunted me for as long as I can remember. I've grown up in fear of the final light being turned off as I try to get to sleep. Until the age of 16, I'd beg my younger brother to allow me to drag a mattress into his room for me to sleep on the floor. I had to drag two mattresses in and stack them, so I was at a similar height to him because I was so petrified by the vividness of my dreams. Can you imagine how pathetic I felt? At university, I slept with the television on. I would usually have an uplifting film playing with the hope it would influence my dreams. I still often wake up confused and emotionally drained by my dreams, much like when you wake up from a dream having lost your teeth, so you immediately grab for your mouth to check they're all still there. While my fear is wholly irrational, I refuse to believe that a dream about me boarding a mine cart that descends into a weird but petrifying underworld, which I have to find my way through and end up in a house alone occupied by paranormal beings, that I somehow can't run away from, has any meaning. Surely it's my mind playing tricks, no matter how many times I've found myself in an abandoned barn boarding this cart. I say that, but when I dream about being a professional footballer and scoring in a packed stadium, I wake up and convince myself it's either fate, or I've peered into a parallel universe. (Yes, I am beyond delusional.) My bed is supposed to be a place of comfort and safety. It's physically my safest space, where I should be most relaxed; that or the toilet. Anything threatening my safe space makes me feel anxious and uneasy.

After moving in with EJ, I thought these fears would disappear. I'd have somebody to watch over me in the night and the ghosts haunting my mind would have two of us to deal with if they entered the room. I thought I felt safe. What I didn't account for is how much worse I'd feel in her absence. Imagine. Still, at the age of 24, with the landing light switched on so I can see it shining through the bottom of the door. This lets me know if any trespasser is waiting on the other side to break in. I also leave the television on, glowing in the corner with a film I've seen scores of times to act as comfort. I don't sleep; I stare at the door until my body shuts itself down and my nightmares begin.

On a cold December night in 2017, I was alone for the evening while EJ worked a night shift, though my thoughts were providing good company as usual. I was with my best friend, me. I decided to take my mind and body elsewhere. I went to see the eighth instalment of *Star Wars*, which reminds me, those who think it's funny to Tweet spoilers for any form of entertainment are on the same level as ticket touts.

After escaping to a galaxy far, far away with nachos and an extra-large pick-n-mix, I walked home trying to focus on the feelings of elation I had from the Force. What a story, the franchise I grew up adoring was alive again. I had to focus on these feelings to batter away the dread looming over me, asking how I'd get through the next seven hours alone. Any negative feeling had to be whistled away with the opening theme of *Star Wars*. I knew my excitement would win the battle, just as the Jedi had won. I underwent my usual routine: light on, door closed, TV on and there I was, lying in bed ashamed of how excited I was over a Star Wars film. I was almost too giddy to sleep because I felt like I was part of something; I love it when a film gives me that buzz.

Time continued to pass as I struggled to sleep, wishing the night away. I tossed from side to side and rewound the film to start again on lower volume; nothing seemed to make me tired. I just lay there hoping to drop off at some point. Suddenly, I heard the screech of tyres and a roaring petrol engine coming from outside. This was odd as I live on a narrow pedestrian street. Vehicles can't pass down it unless they mount the curb and are small enough to squeeze through the stumpy bollards that stand roughly one metre apart. The noise grew louder, building to a crescendo until it seemed as if the vehicle was in the room with me. My body jolted in fear. I momentarily froze not knowing why the noise was so loud. My mind kept attempting to reassure me that I was being a fool, this was no more dangerous than the nightmares I've endured all my life. Stop being a little scaredy-cat.

My mind's attempts of reassurance were interrupted as the sound of the engine running was met with an extraordinarily loud bang. I felt the bang as the entire room shook. I shot upright, still no idea of what was happening. A second bang followed, causing me to leap from the bed and dart for the nearby window. There I saw two figures wearing motorbike helmets, holding a cement block, which they were using as a barricade to batter down the door beneath my window. Through sheer panic, I grabbed my phone and ran to the landing. As I opened the door there was a third smash, this time I could hear part of the door break away and an alarm began to siren. I struggled to tap '999' into my phone because I was panicking so much; my years of night terrors were becoming a reality. My heart pounded uncontrollably as adrenaline surged through my body. I had nowhere to flee from my first-floor flat. My head became drenched with sweat and I became super-sensitive to my surroundings. I raced up the stairs to gain a birds-eye view from the mezzanine adjacent to my kitchen as I heard a fourth crash.

The next few seconds were a blur, I only recall being on the balcony listening to the sound of an idling moped engine, staring down at the two helmets; one white, one black, both visors tinted. I barely realised my call had been connected.

"What's the emergency?" pulled me from my trance.

I opened my mouth to speak, but I felt like if I did, I'd throw up. I felt strangled by my own organs. Every pulse in my body was like a shockwave through me. I just about remembered to breathe. My chest tingled in the cold December air. I held it for a second or two, before blowing slowly out of my mouth, just as I peered back down to the pandemonium below. I managed to splurge out a swift sentence.

"Two people are trying to break in. Robbery."

I knew that I was talking too fast, but I felt so sick. As I tried to gasp for more air, I looked down and realised the motorcyclists were going next door; it wasn't my door. The door next to mine is an office door that occupies the ground and lower ground floor of the building therefore nobody would have been in. My knees went weak as I tried to gain my composure. I zoned back in on the lady's voice.

"You're not the first to call us, we have units en route, are you in danger?" "No, no I think they're going for the office next door."

It seemed as though the two menaces were not getting in as their battering ram had failed to gain entry after a good nine or ten smacks at the door. One walked back to the motorbike as they began to shout at each other, but it was muffled behind their bike helmets and the sound of the engine drowned them out.

Black helmet man walked towards the bike and opened the seat to fetch an enormous blade out of the storage compartment. I watched on, despite being petrified as I was so close to the action. He ran at the door and began to slash at it, desperate to get it open. He was wielding a machete and trying to get through the door; I couldn't believe what I was witnessing. I fled inside to triple-check that it wasn't my door. I sat at the top of the stairs and stared, waiting to hear the next slash, or bang, hoping it would reassure me. It came within seconds; they weren't coming for me after all. I hurried back to the bedroom to watch through the slit of my window blinds. By now the ordeal had been ongoing for at least two minutes, but it had felt like I'd been a prisoner in my own flat for an eternity. I heard more commotion as I positioned myself to peer through the slit and just as I set myself, the engine roared again. The last thing I saw was the moped turning the corner and the two men were off. I yanked at the blind to see a battered door that had been torn apart by the machete. The street was soon illuminated by blue lights as the weight of my body returned, I dropped on my bed knowing I'd survived the ordeal. I wasn't to be slaughtered in my slumber, it was over.

Naturally, I didn't sleep. As if I wasn't scared enough, I'd gone from a conscious fear of darkness to a hysterical panic at the slightest noise. The hairs on my neck stood tall into the pillow, as I lay alone, paralysed by fear while my mind accelerated into overdrive. I waited for an agonisingly long stretch of time for daylight to fight away the darkness, so I could allow myself to get an hour's sleep before work. Little did I know this was the beginning of what would be a torrid time.

The sleepless nights became increasingly frequent. I could do nothing, almost every night I'd lay there haunted by my wild thoughts. My childish fears grew into real terrors that wouldn't allow me to sleep. The one place I was supposed to feel safe now felt the most vulnerable. I couldn't cope with the two or, maximum of, three hours of sleep a night I was getting. How can a 23-year-old be so fearful of going to sleep, especially next to their partner? I begged to not have these feelings, wishing I could be normal, but I felt far from it. Any sound of a distant engine in the night and I'd race to the window to peer through the blind, eager to see it was not another invasion of the pedestrian street. This exact succession of events would occur four times in the space of roughly ten weeks; the same two motorbike helmets bashing down the door in the twilight hours. The only change was their weapons and approach to getting an unwarranted entry into the office next door. One time included launching a pushbike through the full-length windows after they failed to break through the door again. I was alone for two of the occurrences.

It got to the point where I was looking at other flats to move to. I'd look for high-rise flats on the top floors of communal buildings, which would mean extra security for me. I developed a slight obsession for locked doors and windows. I'd check the alarm was active twice before going to bed, having turned it on the night setting as soon as I was home. I'd stand still on the landing in the early hours of the morning, staring intently at the bottom of the stairs to the front door, waiting for somebody wearing a motorbike helmet to smash it through. I'd often dream of my flat, or home in Liverpool being broken into. Every time I lay on my bed, my heart would pound through my chest and I'd begin to sweat profusely, from merely the crank of a bus engine a quarter of a mile away. When I woke from what little sleep I had, I'd be saturated with my own sweat. I'd lie awake, begging for the sunlight to return and give me a sense of security. This didn't feel normal, this wasn't my childhood fears, this wasn't the scaredy-cat behaviour I'd been used to my whole life. This was far worse; I was uncontrollable. I can't even describe how pathetic I felt, arguably more so than when, at the age of 12, I'd beg my sister to let me sleep in her bed along with my little brother and because it was a single bed I'd have to sleep across the bottom like a dog. I somehow felt more pathetic than that.

The anxieties that kept me up at night forced themselves into my everyday life. I jumped at anything unexpected, from a housefly buzzing across my eye line to any loud noise, especially that of a motor engine. I seemed to be in a constant state of fight or flight, being far more likely to do the latter. The sleep deprivation and constant nervousness instigated foul mood swings that would have me snapping over the slightest inconveniences. I'd attempt to pass them off with sarcasm through a smile. Visits from my family would often involve me being called 'moody', which I would have to absorb and joke off to make them believe everything was fine, just fine. It was far from fine. I felt like I was spiralling out of control. I continued to be petrified and checked the window compulsively through the night, begging for peace. There's no such thing as a peaceful night in London, maybe in Hampstead, or Chelsea, but certainly not in Angel.

This was still where I wanted to be, in the centre of it all, in the mixer, but I shouldn't have been this unhappy. I was about to burst. I'd return home from work exhausted from another relentless day, exasperated by the rush hour tube journey home and dreading another sleepless night. Every time I went for a drink, I'd push myself to make sure I'd have enough to fall asleep as soon as I hit the pillow, then I'd wake up feeling doubly worse, as the hangover anxiety would overpower me. I was embarrassed at how I felt because this all came from an irrational fear of the dark, but how could I tell anyone that? I allowed myself to become accustomed to thinking negatively but remaining positive on the outside.

In late May 2018, an infected toe, which in itself is an equally pathetic injury, stopped me from exercising and I spent a couple of weekends alone on the sofa, watching Marvel films to help me escape to a world far better than my own. Films themselves have superpowers, for they can transport us to different universes but still feel so human despite what is on screen. I'd stopped playing football, I'd stopped enjoying anything and I continued to lie awake every night. I felt like I was losing my smile.

Pathetic – I hate myself

During one of my foul moods on a Sunday afternoon, I'd moaned that I never eat spicy food because EJ wasn't particularly keen on hot spices as I pretend to be. In reality, my forehead oozes sweat, and my nose floods from a hot Nando's, but I claim to enjoy it. To appease me she offered to cook a curry that week, one of my favourites accompanied with the entire orchestra: poppadums with mango chutney starters, naan bread, and basmati rice. She was willing to go all out for me. Being a male, therefore by definition being an idiot, I could not realise the selflessness of this offer, not that it was a one-off. We agreed to have it on Thursday so I had all week to look forward to it. Given the warmth I feel when I please her, no doubt, she was looking forward to getting through this meal, given how miserable I was at the time.

Thursday arrived. As usual, I was at work, dreaming of being elsewhere, when my dear colleague messaged me the damning question for anybody when they have dinner plans: "Beer after?"

Given the sun was out, I had zero reason to say no, a couple of beers to help me relax and hopefully after a giant feast thanks to my dearest, I'd be straight into a snooze without staring at the wall for six hours. I'd be straight asleep and rested for the weekend ahead, perfect.

"Go on then."

I even sent a message back home to alert EJ that I was going to have exactly two pints, no more, no less, then I'd return for dinner and an evening with her.

Two beers quickly turned into three, then came another two, so I pushed dinner back to eight thirty, before having one, two and eventually three for the road. I'd ended up having about seven, or eight pints – no this isn't me showing off, quite the opposite. Being the lightweight I am and having not eaten since lunch, I'd found myself incapable of making sensible decisions. My body went into drunken autopilot, as I was no longer able to think. The chemical effect of the lager that had taken over and my body had hit the reset switch. I had to refuel, get home and sleep. Remember the American cuisine that lies within 200 paces of my home? It's a booby trap for drunkards. It is almost impossible to pass the Golden Arches without being sucked in, like a black hole, only it spits you out with ten-or-so pounds' worth of burger meals and 20 nuggets. I returned with my American takeaway late into the evening; stumbling through the door and straight up the stairs to the landing, where halfway up I caught the most ferocious of stares.

She'd deployed her death stare. Not even the alcohol could stop me feeling like I was staring down the barrel of a loaded gun waiting for the trigger to be pulled. As if it couldn't get any worse, with my next step, my toe clipped the edge of the staircase and my large Coke flew out of my hand, almost in slow motion and the contents of the cup emptied all over the beige carpet. Just like that, I'd given myself a death sentence. EJ used words I hadn't heard from her before, she fumed at me with wave after wave of anger. How dare I do this to her, she couldn't believe I'd be so selfish. Why would I act like this? I had no right to use my feelings of late as an excuse for being so self-centred. As usual, she was correct. I binned the McDonald's straight away thinking it would repair the damage, before grabbing my bowl of rice to add curry from the slow cooker, spilling it all over the kitchen side and myself. I had to enjoy it in front of her to calm her down. I took one bite and it bounced in my stomach. I threw the bowl onto the coffee table and ran for the toilet. I then proceeded to throw up uncontrollably in the darkened bathroom, which is my final memory of the evening. Lightweight. Though looking back, I blame the curry.

I woke up the next morning feeling the worst hangover dread. My frosted pint glass had been emptied during the night so I had to climb the stairs to the kitchen, to fetch myself water. My lips were so dry they'd cracked; I needed water desperately. I crawled up the stairs like a gremlin and moved into the open-plan floor; glancing at the oven's clock as I made a beeline for the fridge and the water purifier. It was just six o'clock; no chance of me getting back to sleep. I clutched the water pitcher in one hand and my pint glass in the other, refilling my body with one motion and then the glass with another. I was inhaling the water to rehydrate, desperate to feel human again. After three glasses, the cold water burned my forehead; brain-freeze. I placed both jug and glass on the worktop and pressed my palm into my forehead to soothe the pain; definitely hungover, work was going to be joyful.

As the freezing burn faded, I noticed the bin cupboard was ajar with a brown paper bag poking out. I was hit with a flashback from the night before. What had I done? What I haven't told you is that this was the second McDonald's-themed incident in three weeks. The first time occurring after I'd fallen asleep on our sofa with the drink in between my legs after another Thursday night drinking. The Coke ended up all over our sofa and duck-egg blue rug. That morning I genuinely feared for my life when EJ pushed me down the stairs, this morning a couple of weeks later felt different. The depressing effects of alcohol began to work their dark magic over me. Was I out of control? I wouldn't say so, but I was acting totally out of character, being so selfish. I sat on the sofa holding my head as I heard the bedroom door waft open from downstairs, it was time to face the aftermath head-on. I could hear EJ's slippers shuffle as I sat, in nothing but pyjama shorts, waiting for an earful.

I barely remember what came out of her mouth; her tone was both commanding and fair. I knew I'd done wrong, it wasn't the first time but it had to be the last. I stared through her vacantly, concentrating on making eye contact to show I was giving her my undivided attention. I just wanted to curl up in a ball and shut the world off. I allowed her to finish her speech and mustered up a timid apology, I had to get downstairs as quick as possible.

I felt as if a weight had been tied around my neck, even heavier than usual. I couldn't lift my head as I pulled a shirt out to iron for the day. I yanked the ironing board from the cupboard, making a racket downstairs. I clicked the iron on and stared vacuously through its flicking blue light, as the weight below my eyes grew heavier by the second. I could feel my lip tremble and a swelling behind my eyes. My eyes flooded with water and I burst into tears. This was it. I now completely hated myself. I had snapped under the pressure; London had engulfed me. I was living a life that I desperately did not want to live with a job I was a slave to. I felt like my identity had been stripped from me. I felt so lost and distant from being myself. Can you believe a burger and nuggets pushed me over the edge? EJ flew down the stairs and flung her arms around me. I sat on the bed and yelped like a puppy. It was the lowest moment I've ever experienced mentally, being cradled by somebody eight inches shorter than me, while I wept away my hateful feelings.

How pathetic is that?

Earlier I discussed what it is like living with a doctor and touched upon how I must feel sorry for myself if I'm to get empathy when in pain. Obviously, that isn't quite the case when she knows something is genuinely wrong. In this instance, my cohabitant recognised the position I was in and signed me up to an NHS service called iCope. Through iCope I was paired with a magnificent person who helped me realise what I was experiencing was as natural as a common cold. Through their scaling process, I was told I had severe anxiety and a moderate level of depression, though the anxiety was the main problem. It's so bizarre sitting in a room with a stranger discussing your darkest thoughts and why you think you have them. Through an eight-week process of cognitive behavioural therapy, I tried to source and solve the problem that led to these months of uncontrollable fretting and mood swings. I began to rationalise my fear and tried to observe it. I still have an irrational fear of the dark, but I am learning to embrace, control and acknowledge it, instead of letting it own me. Meditation and an app called Calm have also massively changed my sleeping pattern and general attitude. I won't dwell on this anymore, but seeking help and investing in my mental welfare really turned things around in what was, in the grand scheme of things, a fairly short time frame. I'm able to lie awake accepting my fear as opposed to checking the window with my heart pounding at the faintest of sounds. I almost like myself now as well, though still haven't figured out how to not be a lightweight.

Why do I tell this story?

During my darkest couple of months, I experienced nights where I even lost control of my own thoughts. I cannot describe how horrible it is lying in bed with voices in your head, or hallucinating and not knowing what to do with yourself. I refused to share this with anybody, except EJ, because it was something I was embarrassed by and felt it was so personal to me. I didn't take time off work; I simply visited iCope once a week for a couple of months and completed my incremental tasks set to combat this, eventually getting into a routine. I don't believe my actions were extraordinary, the opposite in fact, and my secrecy was driven by embarrassment. I didn't want anybody to know. I barely acknowledged it. I told a couple of my closest friends when I knew I was managing it and in a much better headspace. Hence, I will make it clear that I am in no way preaching about my story. It is still something I'm embarrassed about how I got there, which is probably why I've found comfort in putting it in written form, instead of being able to openly discuss it with friends and family. (I probably won't ever openly discuss it with them.) I believe that most people in a similar situation to me like to keep their thoughts and feelings in a circle close to them so that they think they have control. Ill mental health can crush people if they don't act. I was so lucky that I was forced into iCope early enough and was forced to do my homework by a medical professional. I've seen how severe depression can destroy a person and it is heartbreaking. It doesn't discriminate or stop with the flick of a switch. It takes time, hard work and support to overcome, and even then it's more about managing it than being cured forevermore.

Anxiety and depression have become the poster child of mental health conditions. They're used as a promotional tool and though people claim they understand the effects of mental health, I'm sceptical. There's a stark difference between having general worries in life and spending months, potentially years loathing yourself and feeling so low that it takes a toll physically, eventually leading to harmful thoughts that can be devastating. There has recently been a headline slogan of 'It's okay to not be okay', often posted online with somebody's confession of their struggles. Life itself is a struggle for everybody; we all experience loss, disappointment and pain. We all need to talk. We don't need to categorise every feeling we have. Not everything has a clinical condition.

The age of offence has promoted anxiety and depression to become a popular movement for some. Everybody has their story to tell when it suits them. It's fantastic that people who've endured damaging experiences of ill mental health can share, but people who crave attention online are devaluing this. They also shift the focus from the many other forms of mental health conditions, i.e. bipolar, autism, or schizophrenia, to name a few. Our World Mental Health Day seems to cast these diseases aside as people make sure everybody broadcasts their own story. I've seen posts about 'a little late-night depression', accompanied with a selfie. This is utter garbage. These posts saying people understand how it feels is like me telling a pregnant woman what it feels like to give birth. Knowing me I'd give up long before labour was even induced; I'd rather endure months of vomiting, swelling, boils, sores and defecating my bed before one morning my body just packing in. How could I even attempt to tell a pregnant woman what it feels like to give birth and that I understand her? The closest thing I've had is being constipated for two days when on holiday in Portugal and I looked like I was at 24 weeks. Also that first colonoscopy we discussed earlier on. I still can't believe the doctor said it was ten per cent of the pain a woman giving birth experiences. There was enough shouting and screaming there, never mind an actual human baby being squeezed out from between my legs.

Of course they don't understand.

Life's become a game about how people or entities can attempt to show they're being inclusive for all and making sure the world knows it. It all feels quite false; another reason I didn't want to tell people about my situation. Another example, my work celebrated the commencement of Black History Month in 2019 by showing *Black Panther* on a screen in the largest meeting suite that sits about 500 people on a Wednesday evening. It felt like a decision made by a focus group of white people. When I left the office that evening, the queue to get in didn't seem extensive. A little off-topic but that film is probably the best original story of the whole franchise, that or Iron Man, obviously. Admittedly, I had no interest in attending, knowing the event would be broadcast through every channel of media possible. Plus it was outside of working hours.

The main issue for people and entities alike is that nothing can ever be deleted from social media. Once it's been typed into a computer or an app, it's imprinted on the world forever. We no longer have a chance to move on. All it takes is one message and the reputations of individuals, public figures, corporate entities, or even charities can be ruined. Everybody is living in fear of the age of offence. We cannot escape it. Even our morning news channels feature agitators pretending to either cause offence or be offended – usually just somebody with nothing better to do. These people get airtime to discuss their bizarre views and promote what they believe to be a controversial opinion, pushing the relatively sane, who are just trying to watch something while eating their morning cereal, to utter despair. Every turn we make seems to be the wrong way down this labyrinth of deceit, from which we have no way of breaking away. We need to break away, even if for a short period; we have to escape.

Let's get out of here.

Chapter IX – Escape

Do I have to be here?

I feel like throughout my life I've endured the present imagining my next step or milestone; being elsewhere and wishing all dullness away. It began sitting in school, wiping my tired eyes during lessons I had no interest in as they had little significance on my life, other than to prove I could regurgitate information in an appropriate method for an exam. I'd slouch in my chair, numbed from forcing myself to learn the moments about a pivot, mathematical differentiation or integration, prokaryotic versus eukaryotic cells, or how Richard III lost the Battle of Bosworth in 1485. He's the man who gave battle in vain. None of this information is relevant to my life now, other than the Battle of Bosworth being the same day as my birthday. I knew I'd never need skills like calculating the area of a circle and if I did, I'd have a computer to assist me. Hence I'd sit in class daydreaming, wishing to be elsewhere. Yet now, what I'd give for a week back in school. The majority of my time spent with friends (I do have some – hello again, by the way) now involves looking back and reminiscing about our best times at school. Unfortunately, there's no escaping the present, but I can give it a go. I must give it a go.

This chapter isn't me attempting to time travel. Brian Cox told me it's impossible as I can't move faster than the speed of light unless I hear a moped engine in the night. I'm pretty sure I've jumped to the window marginally faster. He didn't tell me personally, I attended a talk he was giving at the O2 Arena, and though he did tell me, it was in the presence of 15,000 other people. The talk featuring all things space and time was both confusing and inconceivable, but full of people thinking it would make them smart for attending wearing science fiction memorabilia. Yeah. (No I didn't have a Jurassic Park t-shirt on.) He really tried to dumb it down for us, but it was still too insane to grasp how big the universe is and what black holes actually are. One thing I took away with me is the randomness and preciousness of our planet, never mind my life, so I ought to make the most of my time here.

Anyway.

As discussed earlier, from the moment I leave my front door I dread work (we're there again?), which unfortunately takes up most of my time. Jobs aren't glamorous like we see in films or TV, or hear about from other people. It takes years of enduring a monotonous existence before you can be a master of your own time. We know that jobs aren't as satisfying as the LinkedIn profilers make them out to be. However, they are the lucky ones, who apparently love what they do. That's where I want to be one day. That's where I want to end up. I'm working on it. I am. For now, I must be patient, dreaming away while glaring at spreadsheets across three screens just six inches from my scrunched-up face. This is how I make sure I get my work done, going above and beyond what's required of me to fool others into thinking I'm not miserable and hoping for an extra bit of bonus at Christmas.

It's not just work I need to escape from; it's the world around me. I don't mean to sound particularly sinister here. Everyday life can be filled with such darkness. We're bombarded with constant reports on war, death, and poverty. These reports are necessary, but it's no wonder that sometimes we want to run away. The real world with grown-ups is draining. While attempting to make some sort of living, bearing in mind most graduate salaries are pathetic in terms of purchasing power they provide, our options are limited between everyday escapism and having an elongated escape, which we strive for. This is my poncy way of saying that we need to book a holiday.

Everyday escapism is the simplest form for me and comes through a screen. Televisions are a gateway to another world, any world we choose thanks to the good people responsible for Netflix, Disney, Amazon and the good old BBC (I love the BBC). For hours a day, we can be teleported from our troubles and re-invest our emotions into fictional characters that have struggles we can relate to. They feel so human to us, even if their world can be a fantasy. That's why I fell in love with film, no matter what world I'm travelling to, whether it's a galaxy far, far away, or I'm attending four weddings and a funeral, there is always the relatable human element that resonates with me. As I watch on, I am moved by real emotions of characters in such alien situations to that in which I'd find myself. I don't understand those who claim not to like film or series productions, or any form of storytelling for that matter as I also love getting lost in a book; how could you not love the escape?

We crave storylines. It's why pornography takes up such a large portion of internet traffic with its 30-plus minute videos. People don't just want to see sex; it's as much about the story. (Was it the friend's masseuse mum, or the delivery boy?) We need stories with purpose because we need to escape from our own storyline. It's hard to be my own superhero (or delivery boy turned porn star) when my powers are painfully average. We need to feel inspiration from somewhere. Everyday escapism is a quick fix for that.

I want more

The quick fix, like with any addiction, can only take us so far. We need to constantly have something to look forward to, giving us a reason to get up every morning. One of the more depressing conversations I've had involved a colleague discussing her passion for travelling, despite only getting five weeks of holiday every year. She claimed that she would structure her life going from trip to trip and the time in between was spent looking forward to the next one. Is that the way we all live, waiting for our mini escapes and merely surviving the blank space in between? If such a life was a painting, it wouldn't be a masterpiece. The lady left work to travel around South America and Australia, so the story does have a happy ending. Her story is similar to many. We live from one escape to the next, why must we endure the voids in between? Does it make our escape sweeter? With the world being smaller and events being bigger and better each year, our cravings have skyrocketed, as has the cost of escapism. Glastonbury is the perfect example of this. Between 2008 and 2019, Glastonbury tickets doubled in price to £250. Tickets went from selling out four months after their initial release to 40 minutes. Demand became so high; such is our craving to escape. Obviously, I blame social media for making it more popular.

Glastonbury involves approximately 200,000 people spending up to five nights sectioned into different fields of a dairy farm. Everybody leaves behind the comfort of their homes, beds and bathrooms among other amenities, to sleep in a tent with, at best, a half-inflated mattress while sharing eight compost toilets between hundreds of other tents. You can shower if you pay a premium and queue for 40 minutes each morning; how quintessentially British. We absolutely adore it. It is one of the most magical places on Earth because for five days we become a community that is so distant from our lives outside the farm. We escape paying bills, delivering reports on time, or answering yet another crushing question from our boss with a fake smile. It is filled with such delight, people dancing night and day, seas of flags waving proudly in fields that can host up to 100,000 people watching the greatest artists (at times debatable if I'm being cynical) put on the show of their lives. The stench of the compost toilets, the agonising back pains from sleeping on the ground and replacing showers with baby wipes are all part of the fun, because it's one of the greatest escapes we can experience. By my third visit, I had caved in and paid for the luxury of a shower and a morning coffee, more to do with me not wanting to erect my own tent than anything. Glastonbury has become so popular that parents are hijacking trips (mine included), with me being instructed to never take MDF by my mother.

"You wouldn't dare take anything like that MDF would you?"

MDF. Mum, oh Mum.

I'd like to think it's a positive relationship when you can have such conversations with your mother in your mid-twenties. We think mums don't worry once we flee the nest, but somehow they're always fretting about our safety. MDF was her mistakenly referring to MDMA, by the way. I tried not to laugh in her face, because I know how she feels, bloody acronyms.

I somehow find myself, in my mid-twenties, still feeling overridden with guilt when I'm engaging in something that may not be approved by my own mother. I cannot help the dread in the back of my mind. That same thought of, *What if she saw me now?* much like the defining rave. It's slightly different with dads, they will be annoyed initially, but secretly enjoy a little mischief. But upsetting your mother can break your heart. I must keep these thoughts to myself. I can't be doing something naughty and say to those with me, 'I feel anxious at the thought of my mother seeing us right now.' Can you imagine? My friends already question why they talk to me; I can't give them further reason to. Thus I soldier on pretending to be a free spirit daring to do as I please (within reason, I'm not a lunatic). I believe these thoughts must stem from somewhere, how can I still fear telling my mother at this age? This is a woman who worked herself up to tears over me spilling orange juice on holiday. It was quite a nasty spill where the juice somehow sprayed over the wall. She didn't cry immediately, there was roughly two minutes of 'fuck' and other words that I believe may have been aimed in my direction, before she burst into tears. I was nine at the time.

I'm amazed at the character range my mother has. From moments of utter lunacy to crying at Cheaper By The Dozen. My mum also has the ability to shift accents at the flick of a switch; I know all mums do this but it's still hilarious and needs calling out. If work is being done to the house and the builders are round, the Liverpool accent intensifies. 'Having a laugh, aren't you' becomes ''avin' a laugh aren'-ya', and the woman transforms into Liverpool's hardest mum. Though she is from Kirkby so must be pretty tough. Yet when boarding a flight to a posh destination with a flight time of over five hours (business class obviously), the same woman transforms into an Eton-level of elite, properly pronouncing every syllable and letter that bounce off her tongue. She slows her speech to ensure that her soft accent from her Liverpool heritage is clear for those on the other end of any conversation, her own family included, who, in the taxi 15 minutes earlier, was getting the classic, 'Don't start. Don't fucking start me today, not today, just don't.' She's a real-life Transformer. (Love ya Gorj. Yeah, get over it I love my family. Sometimes.)

Between the transforming accents and my dad's work

laugh, if anything, I've learned to be adaptable. Sadly I am unwilling to change my voice for my environment; this feline will never change his spots. But that doesn't mean I'm not easily influenced. Instead of changing my accent, I'll just spend my free time in the mornings pretending that I'm Detective John Luther, practising the way he puts his hands in his pockets with shrugged shoulders for absolutely no reason or mimicking the way Frank Underwood stares into space engaging with an audience only he can see. I can't help it. It's shameful I know.

(I can still see you.)

Escapes aren't always personal, they are often better when shared. Never have I seen the country I live in as collectively cheerful as in the summer of 2018 – the FIFA World Cup in Russia when England dragged themselves to the semi-final and back into the hearts of the nation. We were lucky to have matches at one, four and seven o'clock with the most extraordinary summer weather we've seen. For an entire five weeks, we forgot about our work, we forgot about our lives, we completely let go and got behind a football tournament and our team. That is the beauty of football; it's a game that exposes our most raw emotions. There is little in the world that can compare to seeing the back of the net ripple after the ball is thundered home by your team. For those few seconds, in particular, we forget who we are and we jump up and thrust our limbs to the sky. I have no words that can describe the noise fans make, but it's such a distinct sound, a unique roar that only football could bring. We couldn't totally escape in this period, however, as we had to put up with the less intelligent of our island nation, who, among the delirium, would smash up bus stops, or mount ambulances; whatever makes you happy, I suppose.

These were halcyon days[6], the nation was united behind the football team, the weather was glorious; the office showed each football game and nobody cared about mergers and acquisitions because the football was on. What more could we want? Everybody was a super fan. It was an adulthood version of our own five-week-long summer holiday. Then England crashed out, we realised football was not coming home and though the heatwave scorched on, the feeling of summer died with one Croatian kick of a football. That is the harsh reality of the world we're in, but to escape for so long was fantastic. Here I am desperately hoping for another in eight years.

If only summer would last forever.

If you think I'm miserable, just wait for this.

Summer loving

If only summer would last forever. Cold and dark mornings are light years away as we're nudged awake by the warm sun each day. The sunshine brings out the best of us; who'd want to be miserable on a sunny day? Even I must try to not be. Holidays come thick and fast and long weekends make the working weeks bearable. My work tends to slow down; all the seniors with families tend to do us a favour and go on holiday with their children.

Our whole lives transform. Gone are Sundays spent on the sofa hungover, questioning if we're happy with life as we watch a romcom eating a share bag of Thai sweet chilli

---

6. My therapy ended during the final week of the World Cup. I was still learning to cope with my anxieties but the football provided the perfect distraction and I think this helped me in ways I cannot fathom. Being lost in something you love for weeks on end brings out the best emotions. I loved it so much, but with all highs come agonising lows and it's managing the lows that I've got better with. I still have them and always will, but it's something I accept, which calms me in a way, weirdly.

flavoured Sensations to make us feel better. No chance. We go for brunch, we go for walks; we're active and love life. It gets better. The beer gardens are open, as are the gin gardens. I'm not certain as to the difference between the two, as both serve identical menus, though I have noticed that gin gardens are often for people who wear long trousers and shoes without socks on. Every other person is carrying an Aperol spritz; people go mad for them when the sun is out. Mad for them. The usual round of four pints of lager becomes: one lager, two spritzers and a gin with elderflower tonic. We've only got to a beer garden and people have completely lost their minds. In London, the prime spot for the Aperol Spritz Society, who are on their Instagram day sessions wearing their Ray-Ban sunglasses and their best but casual summer get-ups, is The Ship. It is an absolute breeding site for the insufferable. Rumour has it this pub is unable to open unless the temperature is above 21°C. When it does open, the Spritz Society comes flocking from all over south London for the day and talks all things grad scheme, now the gap years are over, being a young professional in London and finding their next lover. Why shouldn't they?

Enjoy your life. I must say I am proud to have never been to The Ship despite living in Clapham for over a year. (In fairness, it looks a smashing little venue, I've heard a rumour that Hugh Grant has been spotted there.)

What would escapism and summer be without a getaway? Time to clear the mind, recharge the batteries and spend enough time free from the normalities of life but eventually miss home and want to return with a bucket load of cool snaps. We love to get away from the norm; we need our physical escape as much as anything. In theory, holidays are the perfect escape, be it a long weekend in another European city or two weeks on a white-sanded beach sipping piña coladas by the hour. We are sold the travelling dream and are more than happy to play along. Luxury paradises, exclusive stays, beach huts by the ocean, how could we not be desperate to get there? The thought of being on a beach, or being able to explore a natural wonder to free both mind and body are motivators when sitting through a working week and looking forward to the final Friday of the month for payday. We seem to forget every time that holidays are a lot of stress and admin. I'm not sure how, but I seem to say 'I'm never doing this again' at least once a trip. Maybe it's just me, but holidays can feel less calming and more of a calamity from beginning to end.

Every airport trip is stressful. I've never met a group of people who can agree on what time is suitable for getting to the airport. On one hand, much like my mother, some feel the need to arrive at the airport seven hours before the flight is scheduled to depart, based on no other reason than 'just in case'. Just in case of what, the plane takes off early? No risk of that. Why get to an airport more than 90 minutes before a flight, particularly when only carrying hand luggage? For long-haul flights, I can understand getting there about two and a half hours beforehand, such is the need to prepare for the flight. Plus if you're in business or first class (if only I could enjoy it without feeling the guilt from my parents paying for it), you want to get your money's worth and get to the lounges for a few posh gin and tonics and three servings from the buffet. Yes, I want vegetable soup with four bread rolls, followed by a watery chicken curry, duck spring rolls and the vegetarian option on the side.

When travelling to Mexico, with a connecting flight in Florida, I found out as I checked my bag in that I needed an American visa to enter Miami Airport to then board a flight from Miami to Cancun. It made no sense to me, but neither does America really. Unsurprisingly, EJ laid the blame with me; who else's fault could it possibly have been?

I'd sorted the hotels, flights, packed the bags because I 'do it better', apparently, so I was more than happy to take the blame for this minor speed bump. I'd go as far as saying I welcomed the blame. When handed the application forms, we were informed we had less than 20 minutes to fill them in, as they had to be logged two hours before take-off (good job for my long-haul rule). This was including the section in Spanish. My helpful companion then asked me to translate the Spanish part of the forms. I regrettably informed her that visa forms were not covered in the two years I studied Spanish up to the age of 13. How could I know the translation of the Spanish form when I only know how to say 'hello' (*hola*) or to ask where the library is, neither of which were on the visa forms. It's remarkable how infuriating travelling is with other people. Thankfully, with the help of a lovely woman at the desk, the forms were filled within ten minutes and off we popped to the lounge for our 19 courses, gin and tonics and some extra guilt from the fact I'd not contributed a penny towards the flight.

I could be wrong with my airport timekeeping. Perhaps there is a need to arrive early and avoid any potential disasters, but it feels like such a waste of time as every flight appears to be delayed. Every single flight I take. Whether industry standards have slipped, or planes are feeling the wear and tear from the many flights they withstand, people should realise that flight departure times are more of a best estimate than a punctual take-off time. It's more like a bus stop saying buses come every six minutes (I do get buses sometimes). Airlines still believe that we haven't noticed that stated flight times are suddenly longer than they used to be. They're convinced they have tricked us into believing their flight times are accurate and not actually an hour shorter than they've estimated. When we are inevitably delayed and sat at an airport gate for an extra hour getting grumpier by the minute, they think we're surprised when they announce the expected flight time is one hour shorter. It would be easier if we could just get to the airport an hour later. I assume this is to prevent them from paying compensation to any passengers, which has historically been given as per EU law to passengers who land three hours after their estimated time (though who knows what will happen in the future). I've been on a plane that landed two hours and 50 minutes late on my birthday. The flight time was only two hours and 20 minutes; I took off over three hours late, consequently missed a meal with my family that we'd booked and the first evening of my holiday. I was not entitled to a penny from another garbage flight company that prides itself on being low cost at the expense of giving a woeful service. One would think I learned my lesson after such a flight, but no, the cheap flights to Europe continue; why spend £350 one way to Faro when you can get a return for less than £130? A bit of extra spending money and delays were a one-off, so I thought. Between typing this for the first time and thinking I've been delayed by at least 24 hours in airports. I'm too desperate to get away and too desperate to find a bargain. (I do pay for all other flights, sadly for me. It's only the odd long-haul in my life when my parents have taken pity on me – every little helps.)

It doesn't just stop with airports (I know, I'm so miserable). I have to hope I'm not on a stag or hen party flight. For some reason, stags and hens reduce people to the worst of themselves. People become rather overexcited at the prospect of going away as a group. Stags and hens (from now on will be referred to as 'stens', for lack of a better term) tend to alert the entire flight that they are, as they believe to be, strength in numbers and will be requiring the attention of all passengers, who merely want to get away and relax for a few days.

Recently I had the displeasure of sharing a flight with a stag party to Portugal on a Thursday morning flight. They bounced onto the plane, giggling and cheering as they walked on, again just to let us all know that they were a large group and would be spending 30 to 40 minutes ordering drinks from the trolley, which had about 15 minutes to get down the aisle on the two-and-a-half-hour flight. I say two-and-a-half hours, the estimated flight time was three hours and 40 minutes; we were delayed for over an hour so the flight company thought it would be a great surprise to us that the flight time was shorter than originally expected. Exemplary service. As the stag party took their seats, sniggering and opening their tinned lager, there was a feeling of anticipation among them that was not infectious. Moments later, the stag trotted onto the plane dressed as something daring and imaginative. He walked up the aisle to more cheering from his hysterical friends and the best man announced him to the whole flight as a "slutty Brian May". Yes, as in the guitarist from Queen, but slutty. Crazy. For anyone who's wondering, slutty Brian May involves a frizzy shoulder-length black wig, a black vest and a mini-skirt. If they hadn't announced it I'd probably have assumed it was a slutty Brian May. Of all the people in the world they choose to tarnish like that, why Brian May?

Clearly a cracking inside joke I wish I was a part of. I imagine something witty like 'Brian May-not go to the strip club' because his surname is May, so May-not. Get it? Also, strip club because of lads on tour. Zinger.

It's the same with most stens. It's a head-in-hands moment knowing another insufferable flight is ahead while stens parade with false confidence from their few minutes of much-desired attention. They also feel the need to perform for the other passengers given they have the numbers advantage over those who aren't as fun as they are. We just want to sit there and not shout swear words for the first time in our lives because we've had three pints and a Sambuca in the airport.

They make themselves an easy target. I shouldn't judge people by what they wear (I really shouldn't given my fashion sense), but someone in their thirties wearing cargo shorts past the knee and sensible brown trainers, I mean really sensible and sturdy, shouting all over a plane with his hiking rucksack over one shoulder, tells me he was breastfed until he was at least 13. Overexcited sten attendees like Mr Sturdy Shoes are the kind of people who live in fear of their wives (and mums), therefore get a little too animated when the opportunity arises to spend a weekend away. My natural response is a swift couple of drinks to get me asleep with my headphones in, listening to something soothing enough to send me to sleep, but loud enough that I cannot hear the chanting and cheering. Down your drinks, you gang of lunatics. Once the flight ends, it's a matter of getting as far away from the group as quickly as possible. Why does this always happen to me?

I don't know why I feel the farcical door-to-door trip is worth it. I suppose once the kicking and screaming are over, we're away from it all with the people we love (or are meant to at least) and life can't get much better. Drinking before midday is not only acceptable but encouraged, calorie counting is no more and we're free to do as we please, preferably within a three-minute walk of where white sand meets ocean. The first morning of a holiday washes away any stress of the previous day's travelling; it purges us of any worry back home for we're out of the office and away from reality.

Paradise is coming.

Paradise is heading from the first complimentary breakfast to the beach in our first-day outfits. I am so pathetic I have special (actually a top two) swimwear for the first day. Like a child showing off their trainers that light up, I enjoy showing off my royal blue trunks with floral display to other holidaymakers who stare from behind their sunglasses, silently judging us (me and my holiday crew, usually EJ, my family, or my friends/amigos) for arriving two days after they have as if we've invaded their space. I think other people do this because that's what I do anyway. We'll swan down, books and sun cream in hand, cocktail menu tucked somewhere while we find the best spot. I obviously wear factor 50 because I'm so pale, my skin borders being transparent; if I wore white shorts on a beach I'd be barely visible, like one of those tiny crabs.

No matter the factor, the aim is the same; get to the sunbed and firmly announce yourself to the world. I'm not somebody who trots around a beach searching for the best sun lounger for my Instagram story. Sadly, about 95 per cent of the people I know are those people. Eventually, we'll find somewhere to base camp. It'll barely be past 11 o'clock but I'd like a beer and a daiquiri for no other reason than I'm on holiday and I'm a show-off (I can drink loads, just watch). I love it when drinks arrive in frosted glasses. It makes me feel exotic while I tear through the opening pages of my book, occasionally look up to the point where the ocean meets the sky. As I peer out to the edge of the world, I'll breathe out hard (I do this every holiday; I've perfected this) while basking in the sun for the first time with the entire holiday ahead of me, laying in silence, I'll think to myself, *I'm bored already.*

What's the point?

I'll try persuading myself that this is what I've been dreaming of for the past several months; this is worth exchanging 11-plus hours of my day for a job I have minimal interest in. This is worth spending my days gazing out of a window towards east London waiting for something more exciting to happen. But I'm not sure being on a beach is the cure. There's a possibility that being ginger, I'm not designed to suit conditions where sand meets ocean. Nor do I suit being in the ocean itself. I'm the person who takes 40 minutes to get in the sea because it's too cold. I have to enter through milestones up my body, starting with my ankles, then knees, before the torture of lowering my pelvic region up to my belly button. It's impossible to endure without letting out some sort of war cry, alerting the world to my discomfort. Nonetheless, I'll claim to be enjoying myself, as I stand with my penis all but inverted into my body and unable to lower my nipples into the sea, yet feeling too hot under the sun to not submerge myself in the water. This is probably why so many people spend their trips away texting other people from their sun lounger to let them know they're 'having the best time'. I would try to text friends but I spend too much time trying to mount my sun lounger without getting sand on my towel as well as moaning that sand (or salt, whichever) is inside my trunks and hurting every hole, fold and testicle.

I would try the pool, but pools run the risk of being stuck next to groups of people, which is anything but relaxing, especially if they're British. From the embarrassing fashion sense to the inability to say anything other than hello or thank you in another language, Brits abroad are the worst. What defines us more than anything is the all-day drinking and boisterous carefree attitude that comes with it. No cares in the world as we guzzle pints and cocktails down, getting louder and louder as we tell the rest of the pool about the one care we do have – the price of the drinks. I am a hypocrite yes, but I go quietly about my business.

Speaking of the price of drinks, I can't even go to a shop on holiday without being wound up, as I'll get stuck behind a penny-counter, who empties Blackbeard's treasure from the lining of their pocket to pay for a bottle of Fanta Lemon and a bottle of water with 67 pieces of copper. Don't worry about it; I'll just melt in line while you take north of three minutes to count out four euros and 20 cents.

Here lies the issue. I hate the journey, I don't want to party, I don't want sand in my shorts, I can't relax in the heat, the water is too cold and other people annoy me. I'm not sure I'll ever escape.

I give up. Take me home.

Chapter X – Coming of age

I have always wanted to live as a good person. I enjoy my life (believe it or not) and know that being cheerful is infectious to other people. If people understand my kindness for being false, or subservient, I can live with it. I'll lie awake in the early hours thinking about their misjudgement, but it's a small sacrifice to be happy and make others feel the same. I've grown up with the belief that people are often stupid as opposed to being evil; I learned this at an early age. Being the shortest and the only ginger kid in a primary school class of just 22, I was an easy target for the overweight bully, Faz. I assume he was jealous of my footballing ability at the time (I couldn't let you go without mentioning it once more), back when I was reasonably talented. He'd persist with referring to my height and hair. My sister, Sarah, two years above me would often sort him out on my behalf as any sibling would. She protected me for five years, but when she left for secondary school I had to fend for myself.

One break time at the playground's makeshift football pitch, I was receiving a particularly nasty hoofing from fat Faz, to the point I pushed him away as an immediate reaction. He called me the usual names, but I responded by calling him fat as per my dad's advice. I widened my arms from my sides to make a large rounded shape and said something about him being fat and rubbish. Great shout. I was caught up in the moment, experiencing tiny infant levels of adrenaline, finally fed up with years of snacks being stolen, name-calling and wrist burns. He strolled up to me with his fists clenched and launched his right hand into my left cheekbone. Couldn't have gone much worse really. I'd never been punched before. My face throbbed from the moment of contact. I was only nine, barely four feet tall. I could do nothing but burst into tears. What an embarrassment. I often think of Faz as the first person I encountered who was more senseless and stupid, as opposed to being evil. Not at the time, of course. I hated him and always wanted to be as far away from him as possible. He had his own issues so probably took them out on other kids through his stupidity. Faz and I ended up at secondary school together and were paired in the same form; how joyful. Though his bullying was left behind in primary school, we didn't become friends, nor are we now; there's no happy ending.

Secondary school is tough for most kids. Only a small proportion of people make it through without feeling victim to something. I continued to be tiny until the age of 15 because I was a late developer, which is the worst thing that could have happened in my school (other than making a sex tape like a girl from another school did; known as the 'Very Good' porno). My front four teeth were adult-sized, yet I had a child-sized head so I looked like a little ginger beaver according to some of my peers. Every time I kicked a ball in the yard, someone would always say 'Beaver', or comment on my hair or size. Secondary school was much tougher because there were 180 pupils in a year. It's the first time I realised that life is a numbers game. I had to have as many people surrounding me as possible. For the first few years, I had a limited number of friends; but thankfully my sporting abilities meant that I wasn't a total victim; just a lot of heckling whenever the cool kids were around.

The cool kids were those who hit puberty early doors, the ones who feel the need to show the world their pubic hair and bellow in their low voices, while the rest of us can't say anything without getting called out for not being able to prove our pubes. I'm not sure 'innocent until proven guilty' is a rule respected by playgrounds. I didn't help myself to be fair, attending birthday parties with blue gel in my hair because blue was my favourite colour. Why did my parents not tell me it was such a poor life choice? I remember at my first party being called "blue beaver" by one of the cool kids, which got an impressive amount of laughs considering he just inserted the word 'blue' in front of a name he had given me 12 months earlier. I was such a goodie-two-shoes at the time, focused on doing well in school and feeling awkward at these church hall parties. I was (as we know) rubbish at dancing and too scared to sip any of the four bottles of Smirnoff Ice being passed around 80, 13-year-olds, through fear of getting drunk and not being let out of the house ever again. I'd have a lot more fun on my Xbox than at these parties, so would skip them on occasion to play my online game, Halo, with my Xbox friends (who may not have made the cut).

Nevertheless, I would try too hard to fit in and be friendly with a group that wasn't particularly friendly with me. Deep down I knew I wasn't one of them. I had my own, much smaller group of (three) friends, but I wanted to be friends with the bullies, the men of the year. Another sad thing was I was 13 and there was no sign of a single hair sprouting on my body, despite me checking several times a day. The hardest kid in the year had lost his virginity and I hadn't even discovered masturbation. Being a late developer was both the best and worst thing to happen to me. Then came that special day.

My first pubic hair

For almost three years in secondary school I'd noticed little difference in my body. I was just as short, had only lost my front four teeth and I hadn't a hair below my eyelashes. I'd check daily for any glimmer of manliness and eventually lost all hope. I had accepted I would be a late developer. It's like this was the only thing that mattered. My peers were outgrowing me, leaving me behind like a tiny mushroom in a field of sunflowers with hairy armpits and legs.

Then one summer's day in Portugal, now a moody teenager on the brink of my 14th birthday, I trudged to the bathroom wearing only my pyjama shorts. (I'd even begun sleeping topless like a real man in the hope it would trick my body into hitting puberty.) As I checked beneath my waistband for any sign, I noticed what appeared to be an eyelash had somehow made its way into my shorts. I went to flick it, but it wouldn't remove itself. I pulled at it and to my surprise, it was connected to my body. There it was, my first pube. The fact I'd waited so much longer for this phenomenon meant I got a little overexcited. I was incapable of containing my morning discovery. So how did I celebrate? I ran upstairs and told my parents. This wasn't my wisest move. Whether it was the hormones or the excitement I'll never know, but after years of worrying it would never happen, this was a colossus of a milestone for me. For me to make this discovery in the countdown to my 14th birthday made me feel like Edison with the light bulb or Newton with gravity. I was euphoric.

For a while.

This feeling of euphoria lasted until that evening when we dined with our family friends and my dad decided to announce to the table that I'd discovered my first pubic hair. They have three daughters, each within three years of my age, who didn't find it funny or impressive. I ran away from the table and cried in the play area. I, once again, found myself utterly mortified by my late-blooming. I wasn't a man, I was a boy with one little eyelash. Approximately a decade on and I can relive the announcement at Julia's restaurant. It is one of many memories that will haunt me forever.

I waited for years to show signs of myself growing up. Now I'd give anything to be a five-feet tall, buck-toothed child that was able to commit to playing football or the Xbox instead of forcing myself out to raves not knowing who's playing or what people are taking.

How has it come to this?

Lessons learned

I wish at the time I'd have known the insignificance of it all; popularity, being a late developer, being another ugly 15-year-old. I really was ugly. My four front teeth were far too large for my face, with the middle two crossed over. My canines pushed upwards into the gum like a sabre-tooth tiger because my tiny mouth was overcrowded. I couldn't receive orthodontist treatment because my other teeth hadn't fallen out. At 15, I grew my hair in an attempt to stand out, but it coiled like copper springs growing from my scalp. I remained short and child-like as the boys around me grew into men. At this age, peers have no filter, so the abuse I received, though light-hearted, is engraved in my brain. I ultimately realised the years I stagnated in my physical development were as catastrophic as I'd feared when my own mother described them as my "ugly duckling years". Can you imagine that? My own mother. Thankfully, the phrase was first used after I turned 18, the last among my friends to do so. I'd endured a brace for 11 months, I'd elongated to just over six feet tall and realised that going for the same hairstyle as Medusa wasn't working in my favour. It took 18 (more like 16) years, but the ugly duckling had transformed into a mediocre ginger swan, just in time to flee the nest. Why did nobody tell me that the years spent behind the curve ultimately meant nothing? Looking back, it is now clear that those who hit puberty first were the people who peaked in school.

University was a different experience. I crossed paths with people from all over the country for the first time in the UK and become exposed to lad culture for the first time. It's typically those who aren't from a top city and have spent their youth going into the local village strip that has two pubs and a Vodka Revolution if they're lucky. These people are a different breed.

They compensate for their insecurities, whatever they may be, with lad culture. They'll do anything for a few cheap laughs, usually from the others in the rugby, hockey or rowing club. I couldn't join a university rugby club (not that I can play chase the egg) and be expected to degrade myself beyond belief to get a few laughs and hopefully a funny nickname. To make it clear, degrading beyond belief involves things like being forced into a basement, with all the other first-year students, completely naked, but for a gimp mask covering their faces. Then being lined up on one side of the room as the remainder of the club stood opposite and proceeded to throw a combination of eggs, flour, urine, beer, and anything else they can get their hands on, at the naked gimps (we'll use that name because of the masks). Following the pasting, the gimps then had to walk to the local lake in single file, dive into it and swim around to wash off as much as possible. Having said that, I'd still rather be a soggy gimp than be forced to down the contents of a 'surprise' pitcher and not be allowed to move until it's gone, even if I threw up into the beaker. I'd have to drink that as well, as all the contents of the pitcher must be consumed. That's some people's genuine experience of university. Apparently, it's fun. I thought I acted above and beyond to be accepted in school, but it's not until I left my own bubble and moved to another city when I realised how lucky I've been. There's being up for a drink and then there's, well, drinking your own bodily fluid, regularly. Cool. At least this taught me being well known isn't everything.

It hasn't taken long for my priorities to shift as I move between stages in my life. I lived trying to be well-liked in Liverpool until the age of 18, to trying to be well known at the University of Sheffield, both equally as pathetic as each other but necessary for me to get the attention I reluctantly crave. I don't feel mature having moved to London since university, though my priorities have once again shifted, this time for the worst.

Unfortunately, I've reached the stage of my life where my forehead wrinkles and hairline are constantly on my mind. I have no genetic reason to go bald, but the bathroom spotlights make me rather nervy. I've become so paranoid that some mornings I convince myself that I can feel my hair falling out, despite my barber assuring me of the thickness of my hair every time I see him. Those who hit puberty first in school are looking slightly worse for wear on that front, they peaked far too early. Compared to them, I'm still drinking from a fountain of youth. I just need some Botox to sort the furrows that run through my forehead. The consequences of a lifetime of frowning and over-expressive eyebrows I cannot control have already started to show. I've changed from fretting about why a girl only messages me back once every three hours (despite me messaging back within three to five minutes), to moisturising my face every morning. Obsessed. It is now an integral part of my daily routine, part of who I am and why I take so long to leave my flat every morning. Do I now have to accept that this is who I am?

When I moved to London I thought I'd have it all figured out, 'it' being my life. I thought when securing a grad scheme at a global financial institution in London, I'd reach a point of self-satisfaction knowing that the work I was performing would better my life financially, allowing me to enjoy myself. I thought upon reaching my mid-twenties I'd be living in a sweet spot of being old enough to earn reasonably with little responsibility allowing me to live freely. I'm all but free. I'm trapped in my own mind with nowhere to turn from the overthinking and overanalysing of each action and interaction, finding it impossible to enjoy any moment without the cynic in the back of my mind passing comment. I predict it will only get worse as I simultaneously age while fighting to be seen to 'grow up'. I'm not sure I will find a time in my life where I'll be truly satisfied. Perhaps this is why I force myself to thrust my legs towards the wall every morning and get out of my bed. Perhaps it is why I am able to go to work in Canary Wharf and crave better. I'm addicted to wanting better and this is why I struggle to spend time with those who are content with their lives, or those who want to spend their time vacuously peeping into the perceived lives of other people.

The worst thing about my life is the falsehood I put myself through. Whether it's pretending to enjoy my life through a lens, or avoiding confrontation and acting out arguments in my head for three days, wishing I'd said something else at the time. I know who I am. I cannot change my nature. None of us can. We're each experiencing whatever this life is together as we plod through with our own individual priorities, each with some level of self-awareness that we struggle to cope with. We keep the worst of us inside our head, our darkest thoughts in the back of our mind because there's always somebody worse off. I endure my life in the acceptance that there are many worse off than me, so I've no choice but to grit my teeth (they are pretty after all) and crack on with living my way politely, allowing others to be as free in themselves. You don't need my input because, well, what do I know?

I'm really nothing special.

Acknowledgements

Dear Ellie,

My favourite being. Hoping you don't read this please. Thank you for putting up with my delusions and nonsense on a daily basis. I love you.

Miss ya[7].

Dear family,

I specifically asked you to not read this. Whether you have or haven't, you know how much I love you really. I could write an endless list of things to thank you for, so to keep it short, ta Gorjies.

Don't take the jokes to heart.

To my team in Canary Wharf, who properly supported me throughout the start of my career in the office and in many fun Thursdays (with free drinks of course); you know who you are, thank you.

To my lovely friends (both in London and at home), who have supported me and didn't laugh in my face when I told them I'd written a silly book, thank you.

Lastly, up the GA.

---

7. We're still together.

Sources

TFL Website, page 7: https://tfl.gov.uk/corporate/about-tfl/what-we-do

Behavioural economics – there's a a fly in my urinal, page 41: https://www.npr.org/templates/story/story.php?storyId=121310977?storyId=121310977&t=1633464348215

CEOs called Steve, page 50: https://www.independent.co.uk/news/business/news/ftse-100-ceos-called-steve-ethnic-minorities-diversity-a8769006.html

Russia propaganda case, page 94:

Part 1: https://www.reuters.com/article/us-russia-lgbt-lawmaking-idUSKCN1L51GD
Part 2: https://www.reuters.com/article/us-russia-lgbt-ruling-idUSKCN1N02JY

Kleenex man size, page 95: https://news.sky.com/story/kleenex-rebrands-sexist-mansize-tissues-following-customer-complaints-11528558